40098

D0116381

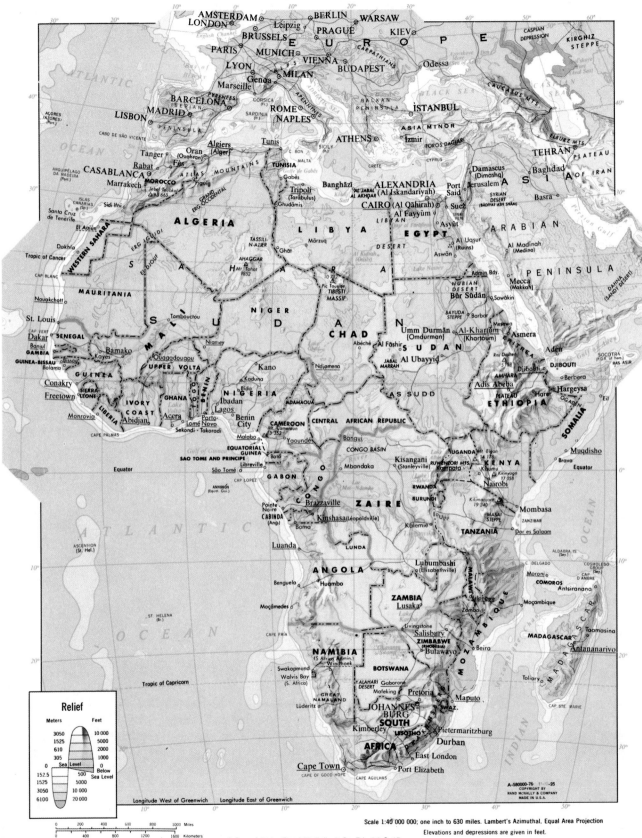

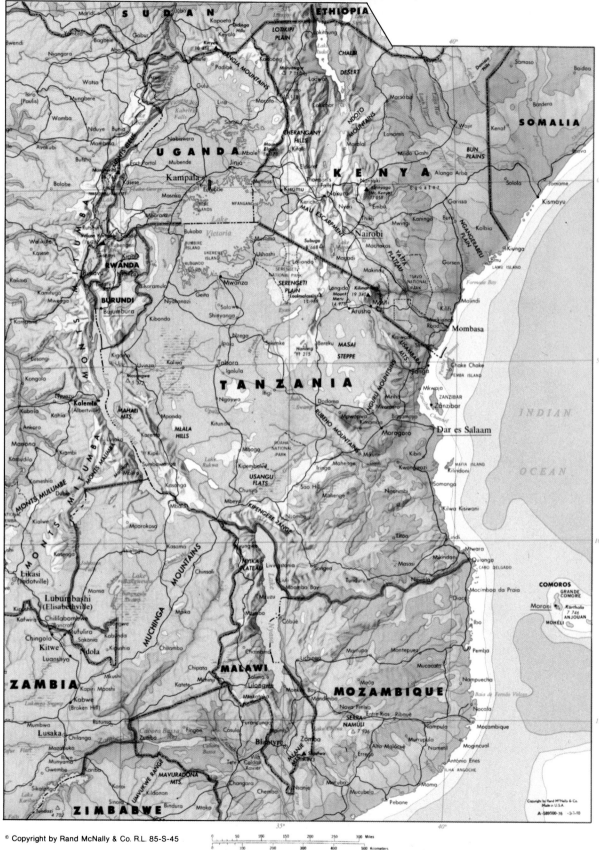

Enchantment of the World

KENYA

by R. Conrad Stein

Consultant: John Rowe, Ph.D., Associate Professor of African History, Northwestern University Department of History, Evanston, Illinois

Consultant for Reading: Robert L. Hillerich, Ph.D., Bowling Green State University, Bowling Green, Ohio

ℚℙ CHILDRENS PRESS ®

CHICAGO

Though most of Kenya is covered by vast plains that support very little vegetation, some areas receive enough rainfall to produce a stunning array of flowering plants.

Library of Congress Cataloging-in-Publication Data

Stein, R. Conrad.
  Kenya.

  (Enchantment of the world)
  Includes index.
  Summary: An introduction to the geography, history, culture, and people of this beautiful East African country.
  1. Kenya—Juvenile literature. [1. Kenya] I. Title. II. Series.
DT433.522.S74 1985   967.6'2   85-14949
ISBN 0-516-02770-0   AACR2

Picture Acknowledgments

Virginia Grimes: Cover, pages 35, 36, 37, 64, 98
Variations in Photography, Inc.: © Eugene G. Schulz: Pages 4 (left and bottom right), 26 (top left), 86, 101
Nawrocki Stock Photo: © Leslie C. Street: Pages 4 (top right), 17, 31 (left); © Michael Fox: Pages 15, 19 (right), 76 (top)
© Robert Frerck/Odyssey Productions, Chicago: Pages 5, 26 (top right), 31 (right), 44, 50, 55 (bottom), 76 (middle, bottom left, and bottom right), 81, 90 (right), 93, 106

James P. Rowan: Pages 6, 12 (bottom left), 18, 103
Candee Productions: © John Ketcham: Pages 8, 109; ©Jorie Butler Kent: Pages 21 (left), 22 (top right), 38, 102 (right)
Chandler Forman: Page 9
Roloc Color Slides: Pages 11, 32 (left), 60, 78 (right), 90 (left), 102 (left)
Camerapix Hutchison Library Ltd: Pages 12 (top left and bottom right), 30, 32 (right), 42, 53, 55 (top), 57, 58, 84, 85 (right), 89
Root Resources: © Ted Farrington: Page 12 (top right); © Byron Crader: Pages 16, 49, 94 (bottom); © Betty Kubis: Page 26 (bottom left); © Lois M. Kransz: Page 43; © Beverly Ausfahl: Page 119
Stock Imagery: © Charles G. Summers, Jr.: Pages 19 (left), 123; © Rita Summers: Page 21 (right)
Colour Library International: Pages 20, 94 (top), 97, 99, 111
Hillstrom Stock Photos: © Earl L. Kubis: Pages 22 (left), 85 (left), 104; © Betty Kubis: Page 22 (bottom right); © Carl Purcell: Pages 23, 67 (left), 78 (left), 96, 116
Marilyn Gartman Agency/Photri: Pages 56, 75
Victor Englebert: Pages 26 (bottom right), 39, 40
Historical Pictures Service, Inc., Chicago: Pages 61, 62
Cameramann International Ltd.: Pages 65, 66, 67 (right)
UPI: Pages 70, 71
Len Meents: Maps on pages 8, 15, 66, 94
Courtesy Flag Research Center, Winchester, Massachusetts 01890: Flag on back cover
Cover: A variety of animals at the Kilaguni Lodge water hole in Tsavo National Park

Two Kikuyu boys tend the family cattle and goats.

TABLE OF CONTENTS

According to Kikuyu legend, lofty, snowcapped Mount Kenya and the beautiful countryside surrounding it were given to the Kikuyu for all time.

Chapter 1

THE MARVELOUS LAND
OF KENYA

At the dawn of time, the Supreme Being, called Ngai, created his home on earth by building a towering mountain. Surrounding the mountain, he forged a countryside so beautiful that it seemed like a garden fit for the gods. On the land, Ngai placed a host of animals ranging from the tiny squirrel to the giant elephant. Finally, Ngai created a man named Gikuyu and a woman named Mumbi. Ngai gave the magnificent land surrounding the mountain to the man and the woman and to their descendants for all time.

This legend is told by the Kikuyu people. The mountain built by the god is lofty, snowcapped Mount Kenya. The beautiful countryside surrounding the mountain is part of the modern nation of Kenya.

A RICH AND VARIED COUNTRY

Kenya, which lies on the eastern coast of Africa, is divided almost exactly in half by the equator. The country spreads over 224,961 square miles (582,647 square kilometers). Its scenery ranges from deserts to swamps, from green, rolling hills to snow-covered mountain peaks.

Lamu is one of the islands that dot the coastal area of Kenya.

The countryside, so exotic and widely varied, is usually divided by geographers into three separate land regions: the coast, the plains, and the highlands.

Kenya's seacoast stretches some 300 miles (483 kilometers). Viewing the coastline from a boat is a breathtaking experience. Along the shore are endless silver beaches, peaceful lagoons, and groves of coconut palms. A few islands dot the coastal area. One island, Lamu, is a place that time forgot. Because automobiles are not permitted, the roads are quiet and the air is unpolluted. To the south lies Kenya's second-largest city—the port of Mombasa. Though some land in the coastal region is suitable for farming, most of it is far too sandy. The climate along the coast is generally hot and humid.

Beyond the coastal region spread Kenya's broad plains. The plains cover about three fourths of the country. They range in altitude from sea level to 3,000 feet (914 meters) above sea level. Parts of the plains are called "the bush" because underbrush covers the ground like a mat. The plains are cooler and drier than

A tea plantation in the highlands, the most prosperous section of the nation

the coastal area. In the north and west, the plains become semideserts where rainfall averages less than 10 inches (25.4 centimeters) a year.

The most prosperous section of the nation is the highlands. This region in the southwest corner of Kenya covers about one fourth of the country. Altitudes there range from 3,000 to 10,000 feet (914 to 3,048 meters) above sea level. Towering Mount Kenya stands at the edge of the highlands region. The climate in most of the highlands is comfortably warm during the day, but chilly at night. Ample rainfall, averaging 40 inches (101 centimeters) a year, nourishes the highlands' many farms. Because of the gentle climate and the rich soil, about 80 percent of Kenya's population lives in this region, some of them in the nation's largest city, Nairobi.

CLIMATE

Since the equator runs through the middle of the country, one could assume that Kenya is a searingly hot country. The climate, however, varies throughout Kenya; altitude, not proximity to the equator, determines temperatures.

In her marvelous book *Out of Africa,* Karen Blixen, a Kenya pioneer who wrote under the name Isak Dinesen, described the pleasant weather in her mountain country home: "I had a farm in Africa, at the foot of the Ngong Hills. The equator runs across these highlands, a hundred miles to the north, and the farm lay at the altitude of over six thousand feet. In the daytime you felt you had got high up, near the sun, but the early mornings and evenings were limpid and restful, and the nights were cold."

A more striking example of the influence of altitude on climate can be found on the soaring peaks of Mount Kenya. The mountain rises 17,058 feet (5,199 meters) above sea level, making it the second highest mountain in Africa after Kilimanjaro, in Tanzania. The equator runs almost directly across Mount Kenya, yet its jagged peaks are covered with snow and ice the year round. On top of Mount Kenya a person could stand near the geographical equator and still freeze to death.

Most of Kenya experiences two rainy seasons. The long rains fall between April and June, shorter rains between October and December. As the farmers well know, however, it is impossible to rely on a predictable rainfall during either season. Droughts one year followed by floods the next are common frustrations. Kenya is a country in which the simple phrase "Do you think it will rain today?" becomes a profound question.

Some arid regions in the northern desert receive only 5 inches

Thomson's gazelles graze on a Kenyan savanna.

(12.7 centimeters) of rainfall each year. The desert air can be so parched that laundry dries on the lines stiff as a board in just ten minutes. The wettest section of Kenya is in the west, along the shores of Lake Victoria, where rainfall averages 70 inches (177.8 centimeters) a year.

FLORA

The natural vegetation of Kenya reflects the variety of its landforms, climate, and rainfall. Along the coast stand groves of coconut palms. Inland, the vast plains are the famous African savannas on which grow tall grasses, low bushes, and occasional thorn trees. Exotic animals such as gazelles and giraffes live on these seas of grass. The savannas reveal scenes of nature's savage violence when grass-eating animals are hunted and killed by meat eaters such as lions and leopards.

Among the interesting plants that grow on the savannas of Kenya are the candelabra cactus (above left), the baobab tree (above right), and the acacia, or thorn tree (below left). Mangrove trees (below right) grow near the coast.

Kenya's stunning array of trees and plants dazzles foreign visitors. One unusual plant that grows on the plains is the candelabra tree. As its name implies, the branches of this cactus look very much like the branches of a candelabra. The thick-trunked baobab tree is also a common sight in Kenya's savannas. This tree rarely grows higher than a two-story building, but its trunk can measure thirty to fifty feet (nine to fifteen meters) in diameter. The baobab tree needs this fat trunk to store water for use during the long dry seasons that are so common in the grasslands. The tree has purple and white flowers and yields a fruit called monkey bread.

The highlands region is a checkerboard of farm fields carved out of the forests. Evergreens stand in the higher altitudes. About these forests Karen Blixen wrote: "The geographical position and the height of the land combined to create a landscape that had not its like in all the world. There was no fat on it. . . .It was Africa. The colors were dry and burnt, like the colors in pottery. The trees had a light, delicate foliage, the structure of which was different from that of the trees in Europe. . . .They gave a heroic and romantic air like full-rigged ships with their sails furled."

LAKES AND RIVERS

From ancient times until the mid-1800s, Western man pondered the question: What is the source of the fabled Nile River that empties into the Mediterranean Sea? Writing two hundred years after the birth of Christ, Greek geographer Ptolemy claimed that the Nile had two sources, both of which lay far south in Africa. Ptolemy believed one source to be a large lake and the other a group of lakes that were fed in part by melting snow coming from a mountain range that he called the Mountains of the Moon.

Centuries later, European men of science discounted the theories of the Greek geographer. How could there be snow so far south in Africa? Then in 1848, German missionary-explorer Johannes Rebmann discovered a towering snow-covered mountain that the natives called Kilimanjaro (the Great Mountain). Ten years afterward, English explorer John Speke discovered sprawling Lake Victoria. Later studies showed that Ptolemy had been basically correct in his determination of the sources of the Nile. How the ancient Greek geographer arrived at his conclusions remains a mystery.

Lake Victoria is Africa's largest lake, a huge body of water about the size of Ireland. It is the second-largest freshwater lake in the world, exceeded only by North America's Lake Superior. Kenya shares the shores of Lake Victoria with her neighbors Uganda and Tanzania. In Kenya, Lake Victoria is known as Victoria Nyanza.

The largest lake lying within the borders of Kenya is finger-shaped Lake Turkana, known in Ethiopia as Lake Rudolf, which is 160 miles (257 kilometers) long. About 100,000 years ago, Lake Turkana was linked directly to the Nile River. Today, all that remains of that ancient connection are the Nile perch that swim in the lake. Some of these fish grow to be giants. The record Nile perch caught in Lake Turkana weighed a whopping 238 pounds (108 kilograms).

Most of Kenya's rivers are shallow and swift running. An oceangoing boat cannot sail more than a few miles inland on any of them. Largely for that reason, the interior of Kenya was not explored by foreigners until the mid-1800s. The country's two longest rivers are the Athi and the Tana. Both flow from the

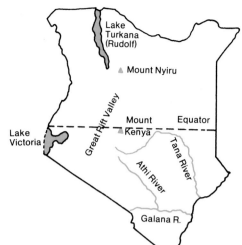

Thomson's Falls is one of the loveliest of Kenya's numerous waterfalls.

highlands to the coast. In the highlands, the Athi divides like a pitchfork and turns into thundering, foaming rapids. From one high hill near Nairobi, fourteen mighty waterfalls, all produced by the tumbling waters of the Athi, are visible.

THE GREAT RIFT VALLEY

A striking feature of Kenya's landscape is the Great Rift Valley, which cuts across the western half of the country. The valley was formed during the earth's prehistory.

This Kikuyu settlement overlooks the Great Rift Valley.

Millions of years ago, a shift between two immense landmasses carved out what looks like a giant ditch. The gouge in the earth begins thousands of miles to the north in Israel, cuts through the length of Africa, and disappears far to the south in the Indian Ocean. In all, the Great Rift is 4,000 miles (6,437 kilometers) long.

In the highlands of Kenya, the Great Rift Valley takes the form of a spectacular canyon. Roads cutting through the highland forests snake left and right to parallel the canyon rim. First-time viewers of this sudden split in the earth gasp in wonder and awe. In many places, the canyon walls are almost vertical. Houses and villages below look as if they were built for dolls. In the flatlands of northern Kenya, the valley is broad and shallow. In the far north, the ancient valley embraces Lake Turkana.

Elephants, weighing from four to six tons each, are the largest animals living on Kenya's savannas.

A WEALTH OF WILDLIFE

Certainly the countryside of Kenya is wild and exciting. During a tour of the country, every twist in the road brings fresh astonishment to the visitor. But the majority of tourists come to see the world-famous wild animals of Kenya. The sweeping grasslands are in fact a natural zoo with no cages.

Road signs in Kenya's Tsavo National Park warn motorists that elephants have the right of way. The signs reflect Kenya's desire to preserve and protect its herds of wild animals. The country's spectacular wildlife serves as a magnet that attracts tourists from all over the world.

Elephants enjoy romping in water, and never roam too far from a river or lake.

All the wild animals that symbolize Africa of old can still be found in Kenya. The nation's savannas, and to a lesser extent the highlands, are the home of elephants, lions, leopards, zebras, monkeys, giraffes, and a host of other animals. In the lagoons and swamps live hippopotamuses and crocodiles. Snakes of every imaginable color and size slither over the ground and along the tree branches. Birds with dazzling plumage flutter overhead.

The largest animals living in the savannas are elephants. Though these immense beasts weigh from four to six tons, they move with remarkable silence and surprising grace. Elephants usually travel in herds. In Kenya's largest national park, a herd may number as many as a thousand. Since elephants eat mainly grass, a herd must travel constantly to find new fields. Because elephants also enjoy romping in water, they never roam too far from a river or a lake. According to a survey taken in the late 1970s, some sixty thousand wild elephants live in Kenya.

Lions and cheetahs are among the many big cats that make their home in Kenya.

Probably no other animal represents Africa better than does the lion. On Kenya's savannas, the lions' sources of food are antelope, zebras, wildebeests, and other hoofed animals. Lions must kill to live. They prefer large prey, but when hungry, they will eat fish and even turtles. It is a rare occurrence, but wounded or provoked lions may attack human beings. During bus tours through the savannas, African tour guides, who are experts on the habits of lions, constantly warn tourists to stay inside their bus and not to wander alone in the bush.

Leopards, too, prowl Kenya's countryside. Unlike lions, who live in small groups called prides, leopards travel alone or in pairs. Whereas lions prefer to remain on the grasslands, the sleek leopards climb mountains in their search for prey. Another fascinating big cat found in Kenya is the cheetah, the fastest-running land animal on earth. In quick spurts, cheetahs can reach speeds of more than sixty miles (ninety-six kilometers) per hour. They hunt in open places, where they can use their lightning speed to the best advantage.

Among the hoofed animals that live on the savannas are giraffes and zebras.

Hoofed animals are a staple food for the great cats. Kenya's
hoofed animals range from the tiny dik-dik to the towering
giraffe. Giraffes prefer to feed on the savannas, where their long
necks help them reach the top branches of thorn trees. Wildlife
experts claim that some eighty thousand giraffes rove the
grasslands of Kenya. Huge herds of zebras also feed on the grasses.
Other hoofed animals that make Kenya their home include
African buffalo, waterbuck, wildebeests, elands, and a host of
antelope large and small. One unusual antelope found only in

Two species of antelope found in Kenya are the graceful impala (left) and the tiny dik-dik (right).

East Africa is the dik-dik. No larger than the average fox terrier, the dik-dik is the smallest of all antelope.

Monkeys live throughout the country, from the highland forests to the plains. Black-faced vervet monkeys sometimes live in city parks or the backyards of Nairobi homes. Baboons also infringe on the realm of man. On highland farms, baboons raid crops. Annoyed baboons have been known to throw stones at villagers who form bands to drive the animals out of their fields.

Huge, fearsome crocodiles live in Kenya's more remote lakes and swamps. Crocodiles feed on fish and birds; they rarely harm human beings. But anyone who comes across a wild crocodile should steer clear of the animal. The crocodile's powerful jaws and sharp teeth can easily tear a man to pieces.

*Among the spectacular birds of Kenya
are the crowned crane (above), the
giant ostrich (above right), and the
brightly colored superb starling (right).*

Another animal often found splashing in the swamps is the
huge hippopotamus. This great beast enjoys sloshing through
water because its buoyancy eases the strain the animal's immense
weight creates on its legs.

Bird life in Kenya abounds. The crowned crane, a showy East
African bird, is found everywhere in the country. Its face is half-
pink and half-black and it wears a crown of spindly yellow
feathers. About twenty-five species of tiny starlings make their
nests in Kenya. Some have colors so dazzling that they look like
tiny flying jewels. Giant ostriches peck about the ground in the

Flamingos gather at Lake Nakuru.

savannas near grazing zebras and antelope. One of the most
spectacular sights a visitor to Kenya can behold is the flight of a
flock of flamingos. Flamingos gather at lakes, where they feed on
small fish. Flocks at Kenya's Lake Nakuru can number more than
a million birds. When that many flamingos take off from the
water, the rumble of flapping wings can be heard for miles. In
flight, flocks of flamingos resemble a pink cloud crossing the sky.

There is a marvelous underwater world off the country's coast.
The long and virtually unbroken coral reef that lies just a few
hundred yards off Kenya's beaches shelters a treasure trove of

marine life. The coral fringes provide a haven for an amazing variety of fish and other water creatures. Glass-bottomed tour boats that ply these waters provide a spectacular view of this underwater world. Some of the more interesting sea animals are starfish marked in red and white, stonefish that look like slow-moving rocks, drifting jellyfish, and spindly sea urchins. One brilliantly colored fish is called the red fire fish. Its colors are so glowing that skin divers are tempted to reach out and touch it. But its stunningly beautiful spines are poisonous to the touch.

THE SADLY DWINDLING HERDS

In 1903, a Kenya newcomer named Meinertzhagen witnessed an elephant migration. He left us this description: "Creeping up a small gully, I found myself but 60-80 yards off this huge stream of moving elephants, going very slowly, sometimes in groups of eight or ten, sometimes two or three. . . .I could see no end to the moving mass, each following the other's trail. I tried in vain to count them. . . .I shall never again see anything like that."

And neither will anyone else. The human population of Kenya is growing at a rate exceeding that of almost any other nation on earth. In Kenya, as in the rest of the world, more human beings means room for fewer wild animals.

Traditionally, man has regarded wild animals as meat, menace, or sport. Hunters have played a major part in devastating what once were thought to be Kenya's inexhaustible herds of wild animals. Early in Kenya's history, hunters—African and European—slaughtered animals at will. European hunters left journals proudly declaring, "Bagged two rhinos today." Or, "We were lucky and shot five lions yesterday before noon." Many hunters took home only the heads of the animals and left the bodies to rot.

More recently, Kenya has led all other African nations in protecting its wildlife from hunters. In the 1940s and 1950s, the government passed a series of laws restricting hunting. In 1977, Kenya forbade hunting altogether. Only in the mid-1980s did the government issue hunting licenses on a selective basis. The government decided to allow limited hunting in order to raise revenue and to thin out some herds whose numbers were growing faster than their food supply.

Hunters are not the only enemy Kenya's wild animals must face. The country's booming human population means a constant encroachment by man onto the territory wild animals need for their survival.

Elephants have always had to migrate hundreds of miles to find enough grass to eat. But today's elephants are denied access to many of their grazing areas. Farmers have enclosed fields with barbed wire, blocking off grasslands where elephants used to roam freely. When the elephants do arrive at a former feeding ground, they often find that the grass has already been eaten by man's cattle. Dozens of other man-made hazards threaten animal life. Zebras blunder onto highways; more are killed by speeding cars than were brought down by hunters two decades ago. Galloping giraffes break their necks on the telephone wires that now crisscross Kenya's grasslands.

In an attempt to provide enough vital living space for its animals, Kenya has built a magnificent system of national parks. The parks ensure the survival of Kenyan wildlife, at least on a limited scale. Even so, the astonishing numbers of wild animals that once roamed the savannas have been drastically reduced.

Among Kenya's forty or so ethnic groups are the Kamba (above left),
Swahili (above right), Samburu (below left), and Turkana (below right).

Chapter 2

THE PEOPLE OF KENYA

The 1985 estimated population of Kenya stood at 20,373,000. About 98 percent of those people were black Africans. Asians, whites, and Arabs also live in the country.

The blacks are members of various culture groups that are sometimes called tribes. Many people object to the term *tribe* because it carries an image of a small band of men and women who live under primitive conditions. In truth, African culture groups are highly complicated societies that can number in the millions of people. Each group shares a political unity, a similar language, and a common ancestor. The diversity of its many ethnic groups has given Africa a rich cultural heritage.

AFRICANS AND THE COLONIAL EXPERIENCE

The current borders of the African countries south of the Sahara Desert were made not by African people, but by white Europeans negotiating in the capitals of the Old World. In the nineteenth century, European powers carved up Africa and claimed large territories of the continent as their colonies. This period of European domination, which lasted roughly from 1885 to 1960, was called Africa's colonial era.

During this period, no consideration was given to the differences among the people living there. People who had been enemies for centuries suddenly found they were citizens of the same colony. When Europeans later relinquished their power over Africa, the newly independent nations inherited the old borders that had thrown together people who had little in common.

Today there are about forty separate ethnic groups living in Kenya. Many groups speak different languages. Each occupies a traditional territory that it guards zealously. Bringing all of these people under one national roof has been the most difficult challenge the Kenyan government has had to face.

THE AFRICAN FAMILY

An African views his culture group as a large, extended family, or clan. All members are considered brothers and sisters. They freely give up their individual rights in favor of the rights of the group. If a farming clan experiences bountiful crops, everyone celebrates. If it has a bad year, gloom fills the hearts of all.

The benefits of clan loyalty are enormous. The sick are cared for, the old people remain a vital part of the community, and no one goes homeless. In the past, this culture-group organization provided a defense against outsiders. Today, clan members look to their leaders to pressure the national government into making laws favorable to their interests.

Despite the positive elements of group loyalty, the old system has divided the people of Kenya. A Maasai considers himself as different from a Kikuyu as an Englishman feels different from a Russian, in spite of the fact that both Maasai and Kikuyu are citizens of Kenya.

The pressures of modern times are changing some of the most cherished habits of the groups. The old close-knit clans lived in rural areas. But the Kenyan countryside is swiftly becoming crowded. Farmers no longer have a wealth of land to give to their sons. Herdsmen cannot find enough empty grassland to graze their animals. Because of these pressures, many young people migrate to the cities, where they lose their ancient ties to the group. The national government of Kenya discourages the people from expressing their age-old local loyalties; instead, it promotes loyalty to the nation.

Nevertheless, some Kenyans stubbornly cling to their old ways of life. Their ancient routines and rituals make the study of the Kenyan people a rich experience. Among the more significant and interesting of Kenya's culture groups are the Kikuyu, the Luo, the Maasai, the Turkana, the Samburu, and the Pokot.

THE KIKUYU

With more than two million members, the Kikuyu, or Gikuyu, are Kenya's largest culture group. The Kikuyu own some of the country's finest land. Their traditional territory lies in the highlands near Mount Kenya. During the colonial era, much of this land belonged to prosperous white plantation owners. The Kikuyu, who are hard-working farmers, raise both vegetables and cattle, and grow coffee as a cash crop. They revere the land they live on. The most famous Kenyan in the country's history was a Kikuyu who took the name Jomo Kenyatta. About his people's close ties to the soil, Kenyatta wrote that the Kikuyu consider the earth their "mother": "It is the soil that feeds the child through a lifetime; and again after death it is the soil that nurses the spirits

The Kikuyu, whose traditional territory lies in the highlands, own some of the country's finest land. These Kikuyu farms are in the Ngong Hills, above Nairobi.

of the dead for eternity. Thus the earth is the most sacred thing above all that dwell in or on it. Among the Kikuyu the soil is especially honored, and an everlasting oath is to swear by the earth.''

Through a combination of hard work and the ability to accept change, the Kikuyu have become Kenya's wealthiest culture group. They have succeeded in preserving much of their heritage, but also embrace modern change. The Kikuyu respect scholarship and expect their children to excel in school. Many Kenyan students attending universities in Europe or the United States are Kikuyu.

When European explorers and pioneers came to the Kenya highlands around the turn of the century, they met and mingled with the Kikuyu. Writing in the late 1800s, England's Lord

The Kikuyu, Kenya's largest ethnic group, number about two million.

Frederick Lugard said: "I lived among the Kikuyu for close on a month. I was more favorably impressed by them than any tribe I had met as yet in Africa. We became the greatest of friends, and I had no hesitation in trusting myself alone among them, even at considerable distances from the camp." In turn, the Kikuyu were eager to learn more about the curious white strangers. Soon, however, the Kikuyu discovered that the whites coveted the land the Kikuyu held so sacred. Armed with powerful weapons, the Europeans forced the Kikuyu from their traditional territory.

Throughout the colonial era, the Kikuyu were at the forefront of the struggle to establish an independent Kenya. When Kenya did achieve independence in 1963, Kikuyu nationalist Jomo Kenyatta became the leader of the new nation.

After independence, the Kikuyu dominated the political and much of the economic life of Kenya. Rival ethnic groups became jealous of Kikuyu power. The most powerful of those rivals are the Luo, who live in western Kenya.

This Luo elder, in ceremonial beads and plumes (left), is a member of Kenya's second largest ethnic group, whose homeland begins on the shores of Lake Victoria (right).

THE LUO

The Luo are Kenya's second largest ethnic group, numbering almost two million people. They are also the second wealthiest and the second most influential people in the country's government. Their perennial second-place status behind the Kikuyu is a source of constant frustration.

The Luo homeland begins on the shores of Lake Victoria and spreads inland. Though their land receives ample rainfall, mountains and rocky soil hinder farming. Still the Luo grow maize, millet, cotton, rice, and sugarcane. Most Luo families also raise goats and a few head of cattle.

The Luo who live along Victoria's shores are skilled fishermen. To them, the lake is sacred. Some Luo and several other groups who live along the banks of Lake Victoria say that a sea monster lurks in its depths. Descriptions of the monster as a giant serpent are curiously similar to those of the one that is said to live in Loch Ness in distant Scotland.

Boat racing is a favorite sport among the Luo. In long canoes that hold a dozen men, they paddle furiously over a measured course. The speeds reached by the boats and the stamina displayed by the rowers is phenomenal. Joy Adamson, the famous British naturalist and author who lived in Kenya most of her life, wrote after witnessing a Luo boat race: "It was magnificent to see the ornamental boats shoot past, the muscles of the crew bulging under their glistening skin, each team working frantically to the rhythmic shouts of onlookers. When finally the victorious crew won the race, by a few inches only, there was such a din and excitement, such dancing and clapping, that it took some time before order was sufficiently restored to award the prizes."

Many Luo work in the cities as mechanics, machinists, and tradesmen. Because they are such fine craftsmen, the Luo dominate the trade unions of Kenya. Smaller ethnic groups often complain that the Luo and the Kikuyu have divided the country between them. The Kikuyu have retained some of the best land because of their claims on the highlands, and the Luo have retained many of the skilled jobs through their hold on the labor unions.

The most widely respected Luo in Kenya's history was labor leader Tom Mboya, who became a leading spokesman for independence during the colonial era. Mboya was a master at addressing political issues clearly and directly. His speaking voice was so compelling that many considered it to be hypnotic. In 1969, Tom Mboya was assassinated by a gunman. The reasons for his killing are still unclear, but his assassin was a Kikuyu. The tragic killing touched off street fighting between the Luo and the Kikuyu. Though tempers have since cooled, the long-standing rivalry between these two dominant peoples continues.

While the Luo and Kikuyu fight for political dominance, another culture group prefers to go its own way. Its members consider themselves above politics. Their roots lie deep in ancient days, when early African men were hunters and warriors.

THE MAASAI

An old Maasai man lies dying in his hut. He is speaking his last words: "I have spoken and acted bravely all the time, and I feel good about it. I hope that my children will be able to follow in my footsteps." This scene begins a book written by Tepilit Ole Saitoti, who is himself a Maasai. The book, called *Maasai*, gives a moving account of the customs and history of the author's people. The key word in the opening scene is *bravely*. The old man is able to die in peace because he has lived with courage. Bravery is more than an admirable trait among the Maasai—it is a sacred way of life. The Maasai people are freedom loving and staunchly independent. At one time, their death-defying courage made them the most feared warriors in all of East Africa.

Today the Maasai are peaceful, for the most part. Their name, reputation, and bearing, however, still inspire respect in visitors to their territory. The tall, muscular Maasai are capable of great athletic feats. While hunting, they are adept at running down wild animals and killing them with spears. A saying among young Maasai hunters goes, "The lion can run faster than we can, but we can run farther." Not too many years ago, a Maasai boy had to venture out in the savannas, spear a lion, and return with it in order to be considered a man. Maasai warriors were heralded as heroes. An old Maasai song includes these words: "Young are the warriors, and we feed them the best of our meat. Healthy they

*One member of this group of Maasai moran (warriors)
is wearing a magnificent lion's-mane headdress.*

will protect our herds from enemies and famine. And they will
stop all the foes of our people from encroaching upon us."

About 400,000 Maasai live in modern Kenya. An accurate
census of these people is impossible, however, because they dislike
being counted and refuse to answer questions about the size or
makeup of their families. Also, the Maasai are nomadic herdsmen.
They drive their cattle from grassland to grassland and establish
no permanent homes.

Maasai women and children outside their houses

Most Maasai live in the area of the Great Rift Valley. Tending large herds of cattle makes them dependent on rain, grass, and movement. The beginning of the April rainy season is the most important event of the year. It means the end of parched grass and hungry cows. "The Maasai know [at the start of the rainy season]," writes Tepilit Ole Saitoti, "that it is time to move their sacred herds to the open country in the Rift Valley. They are filled with joy at the green land and the overflowing streams and lagoons, and listen with pleasure to the symphonies of frogs and crickets. The Maasai celebrate the rainy season with much singing and feasting."

To satisfy their constant search for grasslands, the Maasai often cross Kenya's borders and enter the neighboring countries of Tanzania and Uganda. To the Maasai, hungry cattle are more important than boundaries between nations. One branch of the Maasai makes its home primarily in Tanzania.

A group of cheerful Maasai children

Cattle have an almost religious importance to the Maasai. In the words of a frequently chanted Maasai prayer, "I pray to the evening and I pray to the dawn and I pray to the moonrise. . . . I want a bull with stripes on its neck to add to my herd." According to an ancient Maasai belief, at one time all the world's cattle belonged to them. Because of this belief, the Maasai once were notorious cattle thieves. Though their cattle rustling has been curtailed, even today a family's wealth is measured by the number of cattle it owns.

Tending to the cattle herds is a task for the entire family. Tepilit Ole Saitoti writes: "While still young, a Maasai is taught how to sing to the cattle, to describe the horn formations, humps, and colors, and their little individual peculiarities. . . .The Maasai youth must also be able to tell if cattle are missing from the herd, not by counting them the way one counts money, but by knowing they are gone the way one would miss an absent friend."

Maasai herdsmen tend large herds of cattle.

Cow's milk is a vital part of the Maasai diet. The people also have great faith in the restorative powers of a special drink—a mixture of cow's blood and sour milk. Using a blunted arrow, the Maasai puncture a small hole in the throat of a cow and siphon blood into a jar. The hole is plugged with a clump of dung and the cow rejoins the herd relatively unharmed. The cow's blood is stirred into a vat of two-day-old milk, and the protein-rich concoction is drunk by women who have just given birth, people who are ill, and boys who have recently passed initiation rites into manhood.

In recent years, many young Maasai have moved to the cities, where they have taken up Western dress and abandoned their cultural traditions. But even today, one can occasionally spot in the Great Rift Valley a Maasai dressed in a toga, watching like a hawk over his herd of cattle. Here is the warrior who at one time kept all his enemies at bay. His prowess as a fighting man moved an early European explorer to proclaim: "They are dreaded as

Turkana "giraffe" women (left) stretch their necks with layers of necklaces. This Turkana man taking a noon nap (above) protects his elaborate hairdo by using a headrest.

warriors, laying all waste with fire and sword, so that the weaker tribes do not venture to resist them in the open field, but leave them in possession of their herds and seek only to save themselves by the quickest possible flight."

THE TURKANA

The Turkana are a people who have yet to come into the fold of modern Kenya. Numbering about 300,000, they live in the north, along the shores of a lake called Rudolf in Ethiopia, Turkana in Kenya. Only very recently have these people been affected by twentieth-century influences.

The Turkana are cut off from Kenya's mainstream chiefly because they live in such an inhospitable land. Their territory is a region of swirling sand, parched grasses, and heat so intense that travelers claim "it hits you like a furnace." Early European explorers could scarcely believe that such a large body of water as

These Turkana nomads are watering their animals at wells dug in a dry riverbed.

Lake Turkana existed in those arid wastes. The first Europeans mapped the lake and then hurried back to the highlands to escape the ovenlike temperatures and the swarming flies. Not until the early 1950s did a few Europeans venture back into the area.

Free from outside interference, the Turkana life-style remained undisturbed while profound changes swept the rest of Kenya. As recently as 1969, American journalist Allan Fisher noted the primitive living conditions of the people as he sailed along the banks of Lake Turkana: "Often we saw Turkana fishermen, thin as marsh reeds and naked as eels, standing on the prows of their wobbly, pirogue-shaped boats, tending fishing nets. . . . They would wave, like friendly boatmen everywhere. In a village of woebegone little huts ashore, the Turkana proved just as friendly."

The Turkana are an extremely tough people. To eke out a living in their parched land requires an almost superhuman ability to survive. They are nomadic herdsmen who keep camels, cattle, sheep, goats, and donkeys. They follow the meager rains and lead their cattle to the best grasslands they can find. Unlike the Maasai, the Turkana make few long treks, preferring to stay near Lake

Turkana, where they can supplement their diet with fish. Food is so scarce in Turkana land that the people cannot afford to be choosy. Joy Adamson commented that the Turkana "are the only people I know who eat crocodiles."

THE SAMBURU

In sharp contrast to the land of the Turkana, that of the Samburu is paradise. Though they are neighbors of the Turkana, the Samburu occupy the highlands of Mount Nyiru. The contrast between the two homelands is a reminder of the influence that altitude has on Kenyan living conditions. The mountainside where the Samburu live is surrounded by a semidesert that resembles the face of the moon. Yet the Samburu highlands are cloaked with meadows, green cedar trees, and tall grasses. There is ample rain, and burbling brooks lace the thick fields of grass.

The Samburu are careful to thank their god for presenting them with such a lush home in the middle of a trackless desert. They believe their god lives in a cave on one of the peaks of Mount Nyiru. During prayer, the people face the mountain. When they feast on meat, they place the skulls of the animals they have slaughtered on tree branches pointing toward Mount Nyiru.

The Samburu are related to the Maasai and have the same tall, lean frames. They lead a simple life of herding cattle and raising crops. They have developed a strong moral code and believe friendship to be more important than personal gain. Joy Adamson tells of the time her Samburu friend Lambradan helped her carry a huge plant up a mountainside: "It was a cumbersome plant to carry, some eight feet high and very poisonous, and when we reached camp, our eyelids and lips were swollen from the fumes it

The Samburu occupy the lush highlands of Mount Nyiru.

had exuded. To show my gratitude for his help I offered him a shilling. Lambradan looked at the coin and at me with a puzzled expression, then returned it with great dignity, saying, 'Would you not also help me if I needed help? Why should I take money from you?' "

The greatest problem the Samburu face is that their well-watered, pleasant highlands lie dangerously close to the burning desert occupied by the Turkana. During years of extreme drought, the Turkana graze their cattle in territory traditionally claimed by the Samburu. During such invasions, friction between the two neighbors can explode into war.

In these fringe areas where traditional territories merge, the national government places agents to try to calm tempers before trouble starts. The agents have a difficult job since the government declares that no group of people within Kenya can claim an

The Pokot are farmers who live in the Great Rift Valley.

exclusive territory. So far, the rural agents have had remarkable success in keeping peace in Kenya's countryside.

THE POKOT

Living in the Great Rift Valley is a small but interesting group of people called the Pokot. Numbering about 200,000, the Pokot have resisted the pressure to modernize. They apparently feel that the benefits of their traditional way of life outweigh the conveniences of Western society.

Most Pokot are farmers. Through a complex system of land division, each family tends a garden-sized plot. At the end of the year, crops are distributed so that every family within the community receives an equal share. To guard against crop failures, the Pokot practice a form of scientific farming. Because theirs is a mountainous land, one family's plot might be 2,000 feet (610 meters) higher or lower than another's and therefore receive radically different rainfall. For that reason, different crops are planted at different levels, thereby reducing the chances of a massive crop failure that would bring famine to the whole group.

The Kikuyu (above), as well as the Pokot and other African clans, hold frequent group councils to rule on a variety of disputes.

The Pokot hold a group council to rule on such matters as disputes over property or squabbles among neighbors. American journalist Elizabeth Meyerhoff, who lived several years with the Pokot, explains: "Pokot men, it seemed, always could find time to meet with their friends at *kokwo,* an almost daily council held in a special area under a large tree. *Kokwo* is kind of an open-air court for the settling of disputes."

When Meyerhoff was ending her stay with the Pokot and saying her farewells, she was touched by the words of an elderly man named Chermit who had become her close friend: "I often remember Chermit's giving the words of traditional blessing, each phrase repeated by everyone present, 'The stars are hearing, the earth is hearing. The people are hearing—all is well, good, sweet. Then laugh, laugh, laugh.' "

THE PROBLEM OF TRIBALISM

The Kamba people live in central Kenya. Their northern border skirts the homeland of their former enemies, the Maasai. In these fringe areas, Kamba and Maasai boys and girls attend the same schools. Journalist John Reader gave this account of the events in a Kamba village when a schoolboy innocently brought a Maasai classmate home with him: "How do you describe another man's fear? Makula (the father of the Kamba boy) didn't shout or shake or jump up to his feet and run away. He simply jerked his head toward Kipeliam, the Maasai boy, and asked in tones of almost feminine timidity, 'Maasai? He's really Maasai?' Makula's son, Joshua, nodded. The old man twisted his hands, his eyes flicked to and fro. . . .He was no longer a man politely entertaining his son's guest. Suddenly he had become a householder with a mortal enemy in the compound."

This rivalry between ethnic groups is generally called tribalism. Certainly it is not a problem faced by Kenya alone. The highly respected first president of the Ivory Coast, Félix-Houphouët-Boigny, once said that "tribalism is the scourge of Africa."

African tribalism has sometimes led to bloodshed on a tragic scale. The Biafran War between the Ibo people and their rivals in Nigeria, fought between 1966 and 1970, took thousands of lives.

The Kenyan national government believes that education is a prime key in breaking down the negative aspects of tribalism. John Reader told of a rural high school in Kenya that had both Maasai and Kamba students: "The school's debating society had before it the motion that the schools in Kenya should be tribal. Under a tin roof, crowded on rough wooden benches, following the style of British parliamentary procedure. . .the motion was

45

resoundingly defeated. The summation: 'Kenya is a democracy, schools are not for tribes, they are for the nation. Our children must mix as in a true democracy.' "

With few exceptions, Kenya enjoyed internal peace after achieving independence in 1963. Young people in the mid-1980s had no firsthand experience of border wars or cattle raids, and in the democracy of the classroom they raised their hands together as Kenyans.

SWAHILI

Language is a nagging problem in Kenya. Each ethnic group has developed its own dialect; one can be as different from another as English is from German. The government has attempted to overcome the language problem by making Swahili the national language of Kenya.

The Swahili language has an interesting history. The name comes from an Arabic word meaning "coast." At one time, a group of people known as the Swahili lived on Africa's east coast. They traveled over all of eastern Africa trading in gold and ivory. As they traveled, they taught the local people words and phrases of their language. Because Swahili was already familiar to many East Africans, the leaders of both Kenya and Tanzania chose it as their national language.

Today, Swahili is spoken in most of Kenya's classrooms. Night classes are offered to adults in the rural areas. English is the second most widely spoken language in the country. Nearly all primary-school graduates speak it. For Kenyans, English is the language of technology, medicine, international trade, and business.

One interesting Swahili word—*harambee*—was often chanted by Jomo Kenyatta, Kenya's first president. In a clear, commanding voice the president would shout the word to an audience of thousands of Kenyans, many of whom had traveled hundreds of miles to hear him speak. Like a roar of thunder, the massed audience would echo back, "HAA-RAAAM-BAY." The word symbolized Kenyatta's dream of unity for his nation. In English, *harambee* means "let us all pull together."

KENYA'S NON-BLACK PEOPLE

When Kenya achieved independence in 1963, the nation had the largest non-black population in East Africa. A census taken in 1962 counted 8,365,942 blacks and 270,321 non-blacks. Of the non-blacks, 176,613 were classified as Asians, 55,759 as Europeans, 34,048 as Arabs, and 3,901 as "others."

On assuming office as Kenya's first president, Jomo Kenyatta offered the non-blacks a chance to apply for Kenyan citizenship. In speech after speech, he urged black Africans to be tolerant of white Europeans even though the whites had been their colonial overlords only a few years earlier. "Our aim is to bring people of all races together," said Kenyatta. "We desire to bring love where there was hatred, peace where there was violence."

Before there could be genuine peace among the races, however, some sort of economic equality had to be established. During the colonial era, the white Europeans, who numbered less than 1 percent of the population, owned 25 percent of the nation's farmland. When Kenya achieved independence, many European families fled the country, abandoning their land. The government rented or sold this land to black Africans. The European plantation owners who remained were required to break up their land and sell the parcels to Africans. Only Europeans who became citizens were permitted to own land. Those who stayed were treated with dignity and respect and received a fair price for the land they sold. Though they no longer own farms that spread from horizon to horizon, they are financially comfortable and love their exotic adopted land.

Kenya's Asians have not fared as well as the Europeans. During the colonial era, a power structure developed in Kenya between Europeans (the wealthy landowners who ruled the colony) and Asians (the middle-class merchants who dominated trade). Many black Africans were more bitter toward the Asians than toward the Europeans. While Kenya was a British colony, no African could dream of becoming a powerful landowner. But an African might have been able to own a small village grocery store—if all such stores had not already been owned by Asians.

After independence, the bitterness the black Africans felt toward the Asian merchants remained. Kenya's Asians also formed their own communities, and the blacks interpreted their clannishness as an implied statement of superiority.

In the late 1960s, when they saw their business privileges vanish, thousands of Asians left Kenya. By 1972, almost half had gone. It was a sad chapter in Kenya's history. Many of the Asians had been born in the country and considered it their home. During the 1960s, anti-Asian feelings were exhibited in other East African countries as well. In Uganda, a large-scale Asian exodus occurred.

Arabs make up the third largest non-black minority group in Kenya. Most Kenyan Arabs live near the coast, where their ancestors first began building settlements almost a thousand years

Most of Kenya's Arabs live along the coast and in the port city of Mombasa, whose Old Harbor is shown here.

ago. Kenya's major port city, Mombasa, with its Arab bazaars and Moslem mosques, looks as if it belongs in the Middle East instead of in sub-Sahara Africa.

Although Arab influence is prominent on the coast, it has never extended to the interior. Today's Arabs, most of whom are merchants, remain in their coastal enclaves. Almost unnoticed in contemporary society, the Arabs are, nevertheless, an important part of Kenya's past.

Shown at work in the National Museum of Kenya in Nairobi is the assistant to anthropologist Richard E. Leakey, the administrative director of the museum.

Chapter 3

FROM THE
DAWN OF MAN

Mystery shrouds much of Kenya's distant past. Prehistoric Kenyans left little evidence of their way of life. Because the people who lived in Africa before the coming of Europeans had no written language or calendar, they were unable to record events. Only by painstakingly rummaging through ruins and piecing together folktales have archaeologists been able to unlock many puzzles of Kenya's history.

PREHISTORIC KENYA

Kenya may have been the birthplace, or at least the childhood home, of all mankind. Some of the oldest hominid fossils ever found have been unearthed from Kenya's soil. Anthropologists Louis S.B. Leakey and his wife, Mary Nicol Leakey, began their search for early man at sites in the Great Rift Valley. In the early 1960s, the Leakeys uncovered fragments of teeth and a jawbone they calculated to be fourteen million years old. The fragments came from a creature the Leakeys believed to be an early ancestor of man. In 1972, their son Richard, also an anthropologist, discovered two skulls on a hillside near Lake Turkana (Rudolf). The skulls belonged to a humanlike being that had lived in the area some three million years ago.

The Leakeys' findings have dramatically pushed back scientists' estimates of the beginnings of human evolution. Before the Leakeys began their study, it was generally believed that man had evolved in Asia. The Leakeys' discoveries have led many scientists to believe that eastern Africa was actually the birthplace of man. That region today comprises Kenya, Ethiopia, and Tanzania.

Stone Age people lived in East Africa some one million years ago. Archaeologists still find their discarded tools and their drawings on the walls of caves along the Great Rift Valley.

THE EARLY SETTLERS

Thousands of years ago, small groups of hunters and gatherers called Bushmen lived in sub-Sahara Africa. Scientists believe that the Bushmen once populated most areas of Africa. Though Bushmen lived for centuries in what today is Kenya, they left scant evidence of their civilization. When waves of newcomers migrated into eastern Africa, the Bushmen lived alongside them and sometimes intermarried with them. Today, forty thousand or so Bushmen survive in the Kalahari Desert of Botswana.

Various bands of other early settlers moved into and through eastern Africa. Though some left ruins of stone houses and irrigation channels, eastern Africa remained a sparsely populated region long after the birth of Christ.

THE GREAT MIGRATIONS

A profound but little-known development in world history occurred when groups of Bantu-speaking black Africans ventured southward from their homeland to seek new frontiers. These

Though Bushmen lived for centuries in what today is Kenya, the forty thousand or so who are left live in the Kalahari Desert of Botswana.

peoples may have originated in a mountainous area in what is today the nation of Cameroon in West Africa. Little is known about their early history, but about the time of Christ, they began a trek that would eventually change the face of Africa. In gradual stages, the Bantu-speakers came to dominate each new territory they entered. By A.D. 500, they occupied most of the valley carved out by the Congo River. From there they spread both south and east. Their eastern spearheads crossed the Great Rift Valley where they met and eventually absorbed the Bushmen and other people living in eastern Africa.

The Bantu-speaking people began to settle in eastern Africa sometime near the beginning of the Christian era. Aided by their knowledge of iron making, they were able to support large populations through agriculture. Anthropologist G.P. Murdock writes: "The Bantu have revealed a capacity for explosive expansion paralleled, among all other peoples of the world since the dawn of recorded history, only by the Arabs after Mohammed, the Chinese, and the European nations since the discovery period."

At about the same time the Bantu-speaking people began expanding within eastern Africa, two other major groups of black Africans pushed into the area. They were the Cushites and the

Nilotics. Their migrations perhaps were triggered by a need to find pastureland for their herds. The three peoples met in eastern Africa, where they settled and remain today.

Nearly all of modern Kenya's forty-odd ethnic groups can be connected to one of the three major groups that came into the country centuries ago. The dominant Kikuyu are descended from the Bantu-speaking people. The Luo came from Nilotic stock. And many people, including the Somali living to the north and east, are Cushitic.

CONTACTS WITH THE OUTSIDE WORLD

The one word that best describes the most dominant factor in early East African history is *isolation*. The interior of East Africa is protected by formidable geological barriers. Anyone attempting to reach it from the coast would have had to cross a wide strip of waterless, unpopulated bush country. Anyone coming from the west would have faced the rugged Great Rift Valley, a gorge that was patrolled by fierce Maasai warriors. These obstacles prevented foreigners from venturing into the heartland of East Africa until the mid-1800s.

The region's long coastline, however, presented a far more favorable character.

Arab sailors began visiting East Africa's coast at about the time of Christ. By the 900s, Arab merchants had established outposts along the coast. Important Arab trading centers grew at Mombasa and at the island of Lamu. The Arab people gradually intermarried with the Africans living in the coastal region. One result of that union was the birth of the Swahili people—part African and part Arab—who practiced the religion of Islam.

The island of Lamu, once an important Arab trading center, has retained
its distinctive Arab character, with mosques (above) and bazaars (below).

This monument was erected by Portuguese sea captain Vasco Da Gama at what is now Malindi, Kenya. Da Gama's voyage was the first of many Portuguese voyages of African exploration and colonization.

Largely because of the ivory and gold trade, the Arab cities along the East African coast grew rich. Then, in 1498, the Arabs received an unexpected visitor. Portuguese sea captain Vasco Da Gama became the first European to round southern Africa's Cape of Good Hope and enter the Indian Ocean. Da Gama was astonished by the wealth he saw along the east coast of Africa. He could scarcely believe that the Arabs and Africans had managed to acquire such riches in this remote corner of the earth.

The Portuguese built massive Fort Jesus on Mombasa Island in 1593.

Da Gama's voyage was only the first of many Portuguese voyages of African exploration and colonization. Hoping to get a share of the wealth the Arabs had plucked from East Africa, the Portuguese established their own trading centers on the coast. They also waged war and seized many Arab ports in an attempt to capture the entire trade monopoly. In the 1590s, the Portuguese built massive Fort Jesus on Mombasa Island. This landmark above the entrance to the Old Harbor can still be seen. But starting in the 1600s, the Portuguese, who were always few in number, entered a long period of decline. The Arabs living along the coast united, and after decades of war drove out the Portuguese.

The African people living in the interior were unaware that white-skinned Europeans and dark-skinned Arabs were waging war along the seacoast. Protected by the waterless wastelands and sheer distance, the inland Africans had built a society that was almost completely cut off from the outside world. Most of them never even suspected the existence of white-skinned people.

To the Europeans of the early 1800s, East Africa was only a coast, not part of a continent.

Chapter 4

THE EUROPEAN IMPACT

In his book *Facing Mount Kenya,* Jomo Kenyatta tells the story of a great medicine man, or diviner, who lived among the Kikuyu people just before white Europeans came to the land. This diviner had an amazing ability to look into the future. One night, according to Kenyatta, the diviner made a shocking prediction: "In a low and sad voice he said that strangers would come to Kikuyuland from out of the big water, the color of their body would resemble that of a small light-colored frog (*kiengere*). . . . These strangers would carry magical sticks which would produce fire. That these sticks would be very much worse in killing than the poisoned arrows. . . .He went on to say that when this came to pass, the Kikuyu, as well as their neighbors, would suffer greatly."

To the Europeans of the early 1800s, East Africa was only a coast, not part of a continent. Though the Europeans had sailed and mapped most of the coastline, the country beyond remained a mystery to them. Eventually, greed and curiosity drove the Europeans into the unknown interior, and an exciting era of African exploration began.

In 1849, German missionary-explorer Johann Ludwig Krapf became the first white man to see Mount Kenya (above).

THE INTREPID EXPLORERS

In the late 1840s, two German missionaries—Johann Ludwig Krapf and Johannes Rebmann—arrived in East Africa to preach the word of Christ. They soon caught the fever of exploration, and plunged into the mysterious East African interior. The deeper into the bush they trekked, the more intrigued they became. Stories they heard from Africans told of lakes that spread as far as the eye could see and mountains so high they touched the sky. In December of 1849, Ludwig Krapf rounded a highlands pass and saw what most Europeans had believed to be an impossible phenomenon—a snowcapped mountain on the equator. "I could see most distinctly," he wrote, "and observed two large horns or pillars, as it were, rising over an enormous mountain. . .covered with a white substance." Ludwig Krapf became the first white man to see soaring, snow-covered Mount Kenya.

British explorers John Hanning Speke (left) and Richard F. Burton (right) became the first Europeans to see Lake Victoria, the southern source of the Nile River.

The expedition of Rebmann and Krapf started a parade of explorers, each intent on being the first to see what other wonders East Africa had to offer. Many explorers from Great Britain were sponsored by the Royal Geographic Society. In 1856, the society chose two men, Richard Francis Burton and John Hanning Speke, to journey overland into East Africa in search of the source of the Nile River. It was not an easy trip; as the two traveled through endless grasslands, they were forced to pay tolls (called *Hongo*) to local African rulers, and both suffered from bouts of malaria. Finally, John Speke reaped the reward sought by all explorers—the thrill of discovery. "My caravan began winding up a long but gradually inclined hill. . .when the vast expanse of the pale blue waters of the [lake] burst suddenly on my gaze. It was early morning. . . .I no longer felt any doubt that the lake at my feet gave birth to that interesting river [the Nile.]" Speke was the first European to see sprawling Lake Victoria, the southern source of the Nile.

The most famous of all African explorers was Sir Henry Stanley.

Sir Henry Stanley and his party encountered formidable obstacles during their three-year expedition from the east coast to the west coast of Africa.

Born in Wales, he moved to America at the age of seventeen and eventually became a newspaper reporter. In 1869, the *New York Herald* sent him to East Africa to search for the long-lost Dr. David Livingstone, a devoted missionary doctor who tended to the sick deep in the African bush. After a heroic search through uncharted land, Stanley found Livingstone in a village on the shores of Lake Tanganyika. When the two men finally met, Stanley uttered his famous greeting, "Dr. Livingstone, I presume?"

Stanley conducted other expeditions in Africa, including a fantastic three-year-long overland trip from the east coast to the west coast of the continent. The explorers in his party had to fight hostile local people, steer rafts through swirling rapids, and face starvation and disease. Only Stanley's courage and iron will pulled his party through. Later, Stanley wrote spellbinding stories about his travels. He pointed out that the African interior was a land of awesome beauty with potentially rich resources. The stories gave Europeans the idea that parts of Africa could become their new frontier.

EUROPE DIVIDES AFRICA

As Europeans became more involved in African trade, they gained political control over parts of the continent. By the 1880s, European powers began to stake out claims over vast sections of Africa. Soon there was a mad scramble for territory. The international tension created by the race for African colonies led to the 1884 Conference of Berlin. The conference laid the ground rules for the carving up of Africa. Soon the map of Africa was a patchwork of colors representing British, French, Spanish, and German territories. Kenya, along with neighboring Uganda, became British East Africa.

Certainly many Africans objected to having Europeans parcel their land into colonies. But when the Africans went to war, they found themselves fighting guns with their spears. The prophecy uttered by the Kikuyu diviner had come true. The light-colored strangers from across the big water had overwhelmed the African peoples. But the conquest was costly for the Europeans. The Africans surrendered only after a decade of savage warfare.

By the 1890s, Britain's grip on her East African territory was firm. British settlers began to drift in, and the era of colonialism began.

THE COLONIAL EXPERIENCE

Kenya's earliest white settlers headed for the highlands, where the British East Africa Company trading firm had built several strong forts. These forts spearheaded the British presence in Kenya.

British plans for East Africa included the building of a railroad

This beautiful estate is in the "White Highlands" near Mount Kenya, the area where most British arrivals in Kenya settled.

connecting the port city of Mombasa to Lake Victoria. In 1895, the British began to hire African laborers and bring in shiploads of workers from India. Tracks had to be laid over mountains, through swamps, and across the Great Rift Valley. At one point during the construction of a bridge at the Tsavo River, two man-eating lions terrorized the workers. The 600-mile (966-kilometer) railroad was so difficult and expensive to construct that critics in London dubbed it the "Lunatic Line." Finally, after five years of heroic effort, the railroad reached its goal at the shores of Lake Victoria.

The new railroad attracted still more white settlers to East Africa. In some areas, blood was spilled as black Africans resisted the invasion. The Nandi people of the Great Rift Valley fought a desperate war against the British in 1905. But modern weapons put down each uprising. The white settlers acquired huge tracts of land situated primarily in the highlands around Mount Kenya. Soon the region was called the "White Highlands."

Nairobi, which began as a railroad construction camp,
later became the capital of Kenya.

New towns sprouted up along the railroad line. One began at a
railroad construction camp near a stream called *Nairobi*, a Maasai
word meaning cool waters. It grew from a collection of clapboard
shacks to a town with houses, churches, and tree-lined streets.
Later, Nairobi became the capital of Kenya.

After World War I, the British government launched a campaign
to encourage discharged soldiers to settle in Kenya by offering
them large farms nearly free of charge. The government hoped
both to reduce unemployment in Britain and to increase the white
population of East Africa. Great Britain, which always feared a
black uprising in the colonies, wanted the safety of numbers.

By 1920, enough British people had settled in the area to secure
a special colonial status for Kenya. The name of the region was

65

Left: Kimathi Street in downtown Nairobi
Above: The Parliament building

changed from the British East African Protectorate to Kenya Colony.

The British settlers snatched up the best parts of Kenya for themselves. They farmed almost exclusively in the highlands, where the climate was agreeable and the land fruitful. In Nairobi, they built a neat, orderly city with pleasant shops and restaurants. But from the beginning, the colonists were attempting the impossible—to build a white society in the heart of black Africa. Sir Charles Eliot, one of the earliest and most able of Kenya's British governors, once wrote: "The interior of the Protectorate [Kenya] is white man's country, and it is mere hypocrisy not to admit that white interests must be paramount, and the main object of our policy should be to found a white colony."

Because of their desire to build a white enclave in a land of black people, the settlers created rigid rules to govern their colony.

Left: A Nairobi street scene
Above: The Kenyatta Conference Center

The rules were designed to keep the races strictly separated. A
"color bar" reigned over the capital and all other cities. Blacks
were not allowed in restaurants or hotels unless they worked
there. On trains, blacks had to ride in rear cars, many of which
had no seats. Blacks were required to carry special identity plates
called *kipandes* at all times. In some neighborhoods of the capital, a
black could be arrested simply for walking on the wrong side of
the street. Most of these color-bar rules were also applied against
Asians.

The British did permit church groups to set up a primary school
system that served some of the colony's black children.
Particularly gifted students were even allowed to go abroad and
study in British universities. Many of the privileged young
Kenyans who studied in England before World War II would later
be instrumental in leading their country to independence.

Chapter 5

UHURU

At the end of World War II, the color bar and racial restrictions
in Kenya were as rigid as ever. The black population was nearly
five million, while the white Europeans numbered less than thirty
thousand. Yet the Europeans ran the goverment, owned the finest
land, and showed no intention of relaxing their rule. But the
experience of World War II had a stunning impact on all of black
Africa. Many of Kenya's young black men had served in the
British army during the war. They had fought and died for
democracy. In mingling with foreign soldiers, they had had the
opportunity to exchange thoughts, ideas, and dreams. The
returning soldiers rejected the old colonial system, its color bar,
and its repression of political ideas.

THE STRUGGLE FOR INDEPENDENCE

The seeds of the Kenyan independence movement had been
planted in the 1920s by young, mission-educated Kikuyu. The
Kikuyu were the Kenyans most affected by white settlers, since
the so-called White Highlands had been their traditional
homeland. In 1921, a Kikuyu named Harry Thuku established a

protest group called the East Africa Association. Thuku made fiery speeches urging his countrymen to rebel against the British. The speeches led to Thuku's arrest, and his arrest touched off a massive protest demonstration. To break up the demonstration, colonial police fired point-blank into a crowd of nearly seven thousand men, women, and children. Two dozen protesters were killed. Future independence leaders never forgot this ruthless police action.

One of those leaders was Jomo Kenyatta.

In 1946, Kenyatta returned to Kenya after a sixteen-year stay in Great Britain. While there, he had made speeches and petitioned the British Parliament to grant Kenya self-government. He was a hypnotic speaker and a highly skilled debater. During one debate in London, an opponent argued the old European stance that Africans simply were not ready for independence. Kenyatta replied, "Africans who want self-government are always put off with: 'Not yet. Not till you are fit for it.' Certainly we aspire to be fit for self-government. But we should like to know who is to be the judge of our fitness, and by what standards will his verdict be pronounced."

Jomo Kenyatta's lobbying for Kenyan independence made him a hero in his homeland. In 1947, he was elected president of the Kenya African Union, an organization formed to defeat color-bar laws and to win for blacks the right to vote in important elections. Most of Kenya's people worked to secure their rights through peaceful means. Some, however, chose a more dangerous course.

Secret societies formed by some members of the Kikuyu group began appearing in the late 1940s. Initiates into these societies took midnight oaths pledging to win freedom for Kenya even if that meant slaughtering whites. The oath givers came to be called

In an attempt to locate suspected members of the Kikuyu Mau Mau terrorist organization, police in 1952 rounded up some two thousand Africans for questioning (left). Many Kikuyu who opposed the terrorist tactics of the Mau Mau were given military training (right) so they could help combat further raids and uprisings.

Mau Mau. The Mau Mau movement quickly spread terror and bloodshed throughout the country. A war broke out that, in the end, did far more harm to the blacks than to the whites.

In a series of attacks, Mau Mau guerrillas murdered several European settlers. They also killed hundreds of Kikuyu loyalists who refused to take the Mau Mau oath. The war resulted in shocking casualty figures. Thirty-two white civilians and 167 members of the police force were killed by the Mau Mau. The guerrillas also murdered 1,819 blacks who remained loyal to the government. In turn, government soldiers killed 11,503 Mau Mau and their sympathizers.

Jomo Kenyatta often spoke out against the Mau Mau uprising. During an address before thirty thousand people in August of 1952, Kenyatta declared: "We are being harmed by a thing called the Mau Mau. . . . Mau Mau has spoiled the country. Let Mau Mau perish forever." Despite his stand, many British colonial leaders

When Jomo Kenyatta was sentenced to prison, labor leader Tom Mboya became one of the leaders in the struggle for independence. Mboya, wearing a shirt with a portrait of Kenyatta, addressed a huge election rally in 1961.

believed that Kenyatta was the driving force behind the Mau Mau movement. British authorities arrested Kenyatta, tried him, and sentenced him to nine years in prison.

With Kenyatta behind bars, leadership in the struggle for independence fell largely on two prominent Kenyans. One was the young labor leader Tom Mboya. A Luo, Mboya was a brilliant political organizer. His admiration for Great Britain made his demands for independence relatively moderate. Western countries, especially the United States, hoped Mboya would take over leadership in Kenya. Another powerful political leader was a Luo named Oginga Odinga. A former schoolteacher who had been a rebel most of his political career, Odinga was backed by the Soviet bloc nations.

A fundamental goal among the new leaders was to secure for all Africans the right to vote. In this area, they won gradual victories. In 1957, Africans elected eight representatives to the colonial legislature. For the first time in Kenya's history, black Africans had a voice in colonial government. In an election in 1961, blacks won a majority of seats in the legislature. Also that year, Jomo Kenyatta was released from prison and assumed control of the dominant political party—the Kenya African National Union. With black Africans in power, independence was only a step away.

Also, in the late 1950's, British government interest in keeping Kenya as a colony began to wane. The leaders in London feared that another Mau Mau-type rebellion could break out at any time. It would cost Britain a great deal to put down a new uprising in their East African colony. So, after more than a half-century of rule, London loosened its political grip on Kenya.

A great celebration was held on December 12, 1963. On that day, Kenya was proclaimed an independent nation. Like a roar of thunder, the cry "*Uhuru! Uhuru!*" rose in the land. *Uhuru* is the Swahili word for freedom. The long struggle was over. Kenya, a new country, could take its place in the family of nations.

MAKING INDEPENDENCE WORK

"Now that we have *uhuru,* the next thing is to build a nation," Jomo Kenyatta told a reporter while the fireworks of Independence Day still crackled outside. Building a nation would be no easy task. The threat of violence among the many ethnic groups hung in the air even while the people sang and danced hand in hand to celebrate their new freedom. The whites, who were Kenya's only experienced farm managers and engineers, feared that the enthusiasm for *uhuru* would turn into hatred of whites. The Asians, too, were afraid that the blacks would expel them.

In 1964, a new Kenyan republican government emerged with Jomo Kenyatta as its president. Around the country he was called the *Mzee*, meaning "old one" or "wise one." His actual age was unknown; not even Kenyatta knew his birth date. But it was widely assumed that he was in his early seventies when he became president. Kenyatta's years had not slowed him down, however, and he began the enormous job of trying to make a whole nation from many fragments.

Kenya needed its white citizens, and Kenyatta worked to guarantee their safety. Only weeks after the new black government took over the country, a white government employee complained that he had been insulted by a black African official. Kenyatta telephoned the official and roared in his deep bass voice, "You will now go to the office of the European and apologize. If you do not, you are out." On another occasion he implored a group of European farmers to stay and help Kenya prosper. By the end of his speech, even the skeptical Europeans rose and chanted the Swahili word *harambee.*

To combat tribalism, Kenyatta tried to include a broad range of ethnic groups in his government. Prominent Luo leader Oginga Odinga was made vice-president. Labor leader Tom Mboya, also a Luo, was given a high cabinet post. In addition, Kenyatta traveled to villages and hamlets preaching *harambee* and lecturing against tribalism.

Kenyatta's greatest worry was the prospect of tribal interests influencing the nation's political system. To prevent this from happening, he took harsh, even dictatorial, steps. In 1966, Vice-President Odinga broke away from Kenyatta and tried to form his own political party. Kenyatta felt that such a move would lead to the growth of a dozen political parties based on narrow tribal demands. He ordered Odinga arrested, and banned all political parties except the dominant Kenya African National Union. Because of this stern action, many of Kenyatta's critics called him a ruthless tyrant.

A more serious threat to Kenya's stability came on July 5, 1969, when Tom Mboya was assassinated. At the age of thirty-eight, Mboya was internationally respected as a Kenyan political leader. Had he lived, he would have been a prime candidate to succeed Kenyatta as president. In the first angry days after the murder, street fights in the capital threatened to explode into war between the Luo and the Kikuyu.

When President Kenyatta dedicated a new hospital in Luo territory, his car was pelted with garbage and stones. His bodyguards, in turn, opened fire on the demonstrators, killing eleven people and wounding many more.

The country remained tense until parliamentary elections were held in late 1969. Honest and open elections have been a Kenyan tradition since independence. In the 1969 election, voters ousted two thirds of the legislature, but President Kenyatta's popularity remained strong. The elections had provided a safety valve for the emotions of many Kenyans, and peace returned to the land.

As Kenya moved into the 1970s, the problem of tribalism persisted. Many Kenyans believed that only the personality of President Kenyatta was holding the country together. One burning question crossed everyone's mind, but was almost never uttered: What will happen when the *Mzee* dies?

In the early 1970s, journalist John Reader discussed the possibility of the president's death with some acquaintances. "I put the question to a Kikuyu couple we shall call Dianna and Simon. Both are well educated; he runs a wholesale agency, she

Jomo Kenyatta (left) became the first president of the independent nation of Kenya.

teaches school. 'When Kenyatta dies the Luo will come and cut our throats,' Dianna said. 'We have been too greedy, we have too much. The Luo want a share too, and they will kill us to get it.' ''

The same sentiments were echoed throughout the country. Kenyatta's death, it was believed, would trigger a tribal explosion. Terror and bloodshed would reign. Many Kenyans prayed that Kenyatta would somehow achieve immortality in order to spare the country the horrors of his passing.

Kenyatta died in his sleep on August 22, 1978. A massive funeral was held. All Kenyans mourned his death, but there was no violence. Instead, Vice-President Daniel arap Moi quietly took over the office of the presidency. Ninety days later, Moi was elected president in a general election. Kenyans had achieved a peaceful transition of power from one leader to another. In many other newly independent African nations, the deaths of leaders resulted in military coups and civil wars. But in Kenya, the peaceful transition demonstrated to the world that the spirit of *harambee* had not died with Jomo Kenyatta.

The variety of clothing worn by Kenyans serves as an example of the diversity of cultural backgrounds among the nation's citizens.

Chapter 6

KENYA'S LIVELY
WORLD OF CULTURE

"Ex Africa semper ali qui novi." ("There is always something new coming out of Africa.") This was said by the Roman statesman Pliny the Elder, who lived about the time of Christ. The statement could have been made yesterday. Africa is like a spring from which flows an endless river of artistic and spiritual ideas.

The culture of a particular group of people is defined by almost everything they do—the movies they see, the food they eat, the music they sing and dance to. In the nations of black Africa, cultures are constantly changing. Among Kenyans, culture sways between the old pastoral way of life and the forces of modernization that sweep in from Europe and America. Clothing serves as an example of the clash between old and new. Some people in fairly isolated rural areas wear only a one-piece cloth wrapped around their bodies. Their parents and grandparents dressed in the same way; since they live away from current influences, they see no reason to change. Most other Kenyans wear shirts and trousers and skirts and blouses. Still others have rejected such Western dress and have gone back to wearing the one-piece cloth. They are not unaware of Western styles, but want to demonstrate pride in their African heritage.

About 50 percent of Kenyans are Christians and 5 percent are Islamic.
Shown above are a mosque (left) and the National Cathedral (right) in Nairobi.

The culture of Kenya is complicated not only by the tugs of modernization against the old ways, but also by the diversity of ethnic groups within the nation. Whereas the Maasai spend much of their lives moving from grassland to grassland, Luo farmers rarely leave their villages. Consequently, these two peoples have developed radically different customs and beliefs.

RELIGION

About half of Kenya's people are Christians. Some 5 percent are Islamic. Of Kenya's Christians, two thirds are Protestants and one third are Roman Catholic. Christianity was brought to the country by missionaries who ventured into East Africa's interior at the turn of the century.

Even though Christianity is firmly entrenched in the country, many Kenyans remain suspicious of the religion. Too often in the past Christianity was associated with the white power structure.

Jomo Kenyatta, who believed in God but claimed no religion, once said, "When the missionaries arrived, the Africans had the land and the missionaries had the Bible. They taught us to pray with our eyes closed. When we opened them, they had the land and we had the Bible."

Though Christianity has been a powerful influence on Kenya's culture, it has never fully succeeded in prying the people from their native religions. Even Kenya's Christians still cling to some elements of their old beliefs.

Traditional religions have been practiced by Africans for centuries. Kenya's vary from clan to clan, but some beliefs are common to nearly all the people.

Most Kenyans believe in a Supreme Being or a Prime Creator. However, they also believe that the Supreme Being created the universe in much the same way a skilled craftsman builds a fine clock. Once the clock is running to perfection, its maker leaves it alone. So the Supreme Being seldom interferes in the events of the world he has made. He neither grants favors to people nor demands much from them.

A host of lesser gods and spirits control the vital functions of everyday life. One spirit has the power to grant parents healthy children, another can give herdsmen fat cattle.

These important spirits can dwell almost anywhere—inside a boulder, a tree, or even an anthill. To disturb a spirit's home is to incur the wrath of the spirit in it. The belief that supernatural forces inhabit physical objects is called animism. Because of their belief in animism, some Kenyans will bow their heads and whisper apologies to a spirit before they chop down a tree.

The soul of an ancestor is very important to a Kenyan. Kenyans and most other Africans have no doubt that life exists after death.

At death, a person's soul simply begins another step in an infinitely long journey. At first, the soul might ascend to the clouds or to a secluded mountaintop. But eventually the soul will return to its own village. It might even rejoin its old family in the body of a newborn baby.

A Kenyan who embraces the old religions tries to conduct his life in such a way as to win the favor of as many spirits as possible and to avoid offending the others. Because hundreds of spirits are believed to hide in rocks, bushes, and rivers, a religious person needs the counsel of a spiritual adviser, often called a diviner.

THE DIVINERS

To many Westerners, the thought of a "witch doctor" conjures up the image of an evil old man enslaving a group of superstitious people by threatening them with curses. In Africa, however, a diviner, or medicine man, is a force of good working against evil. A diviner is a mystic who is able to peer into the spirit world by breaking through the barriers that confine other men. Troubled people who believe they are affected by evil spirits consult the diviner in much the same way Westerners consult a doctor. The diviner serves his clients by first trying to find out what evil forces are working against them. Once he understands the nature of the enemy spirit, he provides remedies. He may give a client a charm over which he has uttered a few holy words. Or perhaps he will tell a person always to sleep with his head facing Mount Kenya. These devices are thought to ward off harmful spirits and attract good ones.

The basis of the diviner's power lies in the African's universal acceptance of magic. To many Africans, magic exists just as surely

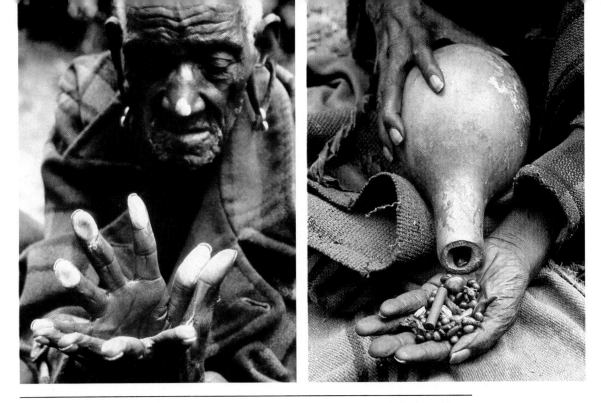

This Kikuyu diviner is a mystic who uses a variety of remedies to help his clients.

as Mount Kenya rises on the horizon. The forces of magic are always in the air, but only a few gifted people—such as diviners—are able to understand and manipulate them.

Even educated Kenyans who respect modern science and medicine do not discount the power of magic. Jomo Kenyatta once wrote, "My grandfather was a seer and a magician, and in traveling about with him and carrying his bag of equipment I served a kind of apprenticeship in the principles of the art." Although Kenyatta had a Western education, he remained fascinated by the practice of magic.

One of the diviner's most formidable tasks is to combat the evil curses of sorcerers and witches. Sorcerers are usually men and witches are almost always women. Though born with the mystical powers of diviners, they choose to abuse their gifts. They use their power to put curses on their neighbors. The evildoers have many weapons. One is a magic bone that can cause people to become ill when it is pointed at them. The sorcerers can also sprinkle magical powder on the doorstep of someone they wish to harm. "At the very sight of such powder men have been known to sicken and die," writes Geoffrey Parrinder in his book *African Traditional Religions.* A person who suspects that a witch or a sorcerer has put a curse on him must hurry to the diviner and hope that his power is greater than that of the evil forces.

When a rainy season has failed to provide essential showers, farmers turn to diviners for help. To produce rain, a diviner will lead the people in a ritual ceremony. Among the Kikuyu, the ceremony involves sacrificing a lamb while the people face Mount Kenya and the diviner conducts a prayer: "Reverend God who lives on Mount Kenya. You who make the mountains tremble and the rivers flood; we offer you this sacrifice so that you may bring us rain. People and children are crying. Sheep, goats, and cattle are crying. We beseech you to accept this lamb and bring us the rain of prosperity." Of these rituals Jomo Kenyatta once wrote, "I wish to put it on record that every rain ceremony that I have witnessed has been very soon followed by rain."

Do diviners' ceremonies and rituals ever work? Sometimes. A diviner often treats sick people by giving them special herbs and roots to eat or to drink as tea. Over the centuries, African spiritualists have discovered the medicinal value of certain plants. Western doctors often marvel at the African genius in herbal medicine. But if the diviner's remedies do not work and the patient becomes worse, the people simply believe that the negative magic working against the patient was more powerful than the positive magic of the diviner. Since in either case the belief in magic remains sacred, the diviner cannot lose. As long as people believe in magic, they will also believe in magicians, and the diviner will remain a powerful figure in Kenya's traditional religious practices.

A PASSION FOR THE ARTS

As is true in Western society, much of Kenya's art is inspired by religion. Through sculpture, music, dance, and literature, the Kenyan seeks to appeal to the spirit world.

Sculpture is by far the most highly developed of all African art forms. Much of what is fashioned by the sculptor's hands has religious meaning. The amulet or charm that a diviner gives a person to ward off evil spirits and attract good ones is often intricately carved. Kenyans also sculpt larger ivory or gold figures that have religious significance.

Wood carving is a widely respected art form in Kenya. Many wood-carvers also use religious subjects for their work. Wooden figures of ancestors are another favorite subject. A carved figure is created not only in memory of a relative, but also as an object designed to please his soul and win his favor.

Westerners first discovered the marvelous African wood carvings early in this century when some of the figures found their way into European art galleries. There they attracted the admiration of many European artists, including the young Spaniard Pablo Picasso. Picasso, a famous painter and sculptor, was profoundly influenced by African wood carvings, some of which came from Kenya.

It is amazing that fine sculpture has come out of Kenya because the nation is the home of so many nomadic people. Nomads cannot easily carry tools or objects of art with them.

Wood carving is a widely respected art form in Kenya.

Consequently, they do not place much value on arts and crafts. In Maasai society, blacksmiths are considered the lowliest members of the group. Nevertheless Kenya, though it has a large population of nomads, has excelled in arts and crafts.

Traditional literature in Kenya consists mainly of oral folktales. Many folktales involve man's encounters with spirits. Some are war stories that heap praise on ancient local heroes. Because no one in the interior of Kenya developed a written language, tales were handed down by memory from generation to generation. Many folktales became songs. Certain groups, such as the Kikuyu and Kamba, may have literally thousands of these songs in their repertoires. Since the colonial era, many of these historic folktales and songs have been written down. Today, Kenyan novelists, poets, and playwrights are developing some exciting modern literature.

In recent years, Kenyans have become interested in Western music—classical as well as rock and jazz. But they still revere their traditional music, which involves singing, dancing, and creating intricate and compelling rhythms.

Kenyan musicians use a variety of instruments, including some made from gourds (left) and thumb pianos like the one on the right.

Although drums play a dominant role in Kenya's traditional music, lutes and woodwinds are also used. The music is polyrhythmic, meaning that different instruments play in different rhythms at the same time. Above the instruments, singers chant songs that have separate rhythms for soloists and choruses. The arrangements are so complex that few Western musicians can imitate them.

The dance is a highly respected art form in Kenya. Kenyans enjoy dancing and watching dances being performed. During dance sessions, even rival ethnic groups momentarily forget their differences to watch each other perform. The dances usually have a religious function. Young women may perform a dance that implores the spirits to give them many healthy children. A farming village may hold a special dance before planting time to ask the mystic forces for a bountiful harvest.

These Kikuyu men are wearing face paint and highly stylized headdresses for a traditional warrior dance.

During the traditional dances, many Kenyans wear highly stylized headdresses and masks that are decorated with feathers and painted in brilliant colors. Many headdresses look like birds, animals, or fish. These masks and headdresses, fashioned by superb craftsmen, are yet another art form in the nation of Kenya.

MARRIAGE AND FAMILY LIFE

Polygamy, the practice of a man having more than one wife, traditionally has been accepted by most Kenyans. Decades ago, when land was plentiful, many rich men had five or six wives. A husband built a separate hut for each wife and a master hut for himself. The system worked surprisingly well in those regions of Africa where polygamy was practiced. As American anthropologist G.P. Murdock pointed out, "Africans have discovered the means of making the institution [of polygamy] work to the satisfaction of both sexes. No woman lacks a male provider. No wife has trouble finding a helper or a baby-sitter in time of need. Custom normally requires the husband to treat each wife with equal consideration, to eat and sleep with each in regular rotation." The anthropologist added that when Christian missionaries tried to forbid polygamy, "the missionaries frequently encountered their strongest opposition from the women."

Today the practice of polygamy is declining in Kenya. The country's Christians have denounced the institution. Even among non-Christians, polygamy is becoming increasingly impractical. Supporting more than one wife is expensive, and overpopulation has made Kenya a poor nation.

A man who finds a woman he would like for a wife enters into negotiations with the woman's father. A sum called a bride price is arranged before a marriage is planned. A bride price might be an amount of money or a number of cattle.

Writing in the late 1960s, Joy Adamson described the practice of securing a wife then carried out by the Tharaka: "The Tharaka are polygamous. The bride price is carefully calculated and staggered: for the first wife it amounts to sixty goats or five head of cattle. For the second wife thirty goats or three head of cattle are given. The bride price is not purchase money for a wife, but is a guarantee of the stability of the marriage and compensation to the wife's group for the loss of her services. When a man has chosen the girl he wants to marry, he arranges for his father to call on the father of the girl. It is the custom for the girl to refuse four times; when she finally accepts the offer, the two fathers start discussing the bride price. The full amount, however, is paid only if the girl is provided by the father with a proper dress for ceremonial occasions. When all this is settled, the bridegroom calls on the girl, and the bride price is paid. Finally, the marriage is celebrated by a feast given at the husband's home."

Today, bride prices are exorbitant. Men who still practice polygamy find they can scarcely afford one wife, let alone two or three. In modern Kenya only the old men who acquired their wives before the prices skyrocketed still cling to their multiple mates.

Whether a Kenyan man has one wife or more, the family usually has many children. Kenyans believe in large families for several reasons. Until recently, many young people died of disease before they reached adulthood. Consequently, a dozen or so children were essential to insure the survival of the family. Also, many hands were needed to tend fields and look after cattle. Finally, Kenyans have large families for religious reasons. The belief in reincarnation is common in Kenya and children are seen as bodies into which the souls of long-dead ancestors can be reborn.

In rural Kenya, children enjoy a life of mixed responsibilities and freedoms. If a family owns cattle, children as young as five or six are expected to patrol the flanks of the herd and chase back any cow that begins to wander off. Beyond their chores, children in rural areas are given a great amount of freedom.

EDUCATION

The government of Kenya has taken great strides in its goal to give at least a primary education to all the nation's children. Before the 1950s, few public schools in Kenya were open to black

Though Kenyan children are not required by law to attend school, 80 percent of the nation's school-aged children attend classes.

children. Black Africans who were lucky enough to receive an education had to attend missionary schools. Because there were so few schools, many Kenyans today over the age of forty cannot read or write. The government has now set up special literacy classes for older people.

Since independence, hundreds of schools have been built and thousands of teachers have been trained. Year after year, education is the most costly single expenditure in the government's budget. Much more work remains to be done, however. Many of Kenya's rural regions have no secondary schools, and some have no schools at all.

Kenyan children are not required by law to attend school. Still, most parents recognize and have responded to the need for education. Today, 80 percent of the nation's school-aged children attend classes. Most of those who do not go to school live in the remote bush areas where schools have yet to be built.

*The University College (left) and the Kenya Polytechnic (right)
are among the dozen or so institutions of higher education in Kenya.*

Primary school in Kenya is a seven-year course. Only the first four years are free. Beyond that, parents must pay a modest tuition fee. The country suffers from a severe shortage of secondary schools. Though children living in cities or populated areas may enter a high school if their grades are good enough, those living in remote areas are often out of luck. The nearest high school might be fifty miles away.

To help provide education in the rural areas, groups of private citizens have set up self-help schools. These schools exist in areas where there are no government schools. The self-help schools are called, appropriately, *harambee* schools.

Kenya's largest college is the University of Nairobi, which serves about five thousand students. The Kenyatta University College is another major institution for higher learning. Scattered about the country are ten other colleges. Some of these specialize in agriculture, others in teacher training.

Though an impressive school building program continues in

Kenya, the country's population is growing at a frightening rate. There are so many schoolchildren that students have to sit two at a desk and share textbooks. Every year still more students apply to enter the nation's already bulging schools.

SPORTS

Soccer is Kenya's favorite team sport. This British import helps to ease the tensions between rival culture groups. When Kenya's national team plays a team from another country, everyone gathers around television sets to watch. Goals and saves are applauded, and no one cares about the ethnic backgrounds of the individual players.

Tennis, also brought to the country by the British, has also produced some exceptional players.

But it is in the sport of distance running that Kenyan athletes have truly made their mark. Runners from Kenya first thrilled the international sports world during the 1968 Olympic games held in Mexico City. There, in the rarefied air (Mexico City is 8,000 feet/ 2,438 meters above sea level), athletes from many other countries gasped for breath. But many Kenyan runners had spent their lives in the highlands or the Great Rift Valley, where altitudes are even higher than in Mexico City. Those athletes grew up herding goats over rugged mountains and walking and running many miles to school. Mexico City's altitude was no problem for them.

In 1968 the remarkable Kenyan athlete Kipchoge Keino started a parade of Kenyan Olympic victories by winning the gold medal in the 1,500-meter race. That prestigious event is often called the "metric mile." Keino, however, had not traveled all the way to Mexico to compete in only one race. He also ran the 5,000 meters, in which he placed second to win the silver medal. In the same event his teammate Naftali Temu finished third, capturing the bronze medal. Temu then entered the 10,000-meter race and won the gold. Also that year, Kenyans finished first and second in the grueling 3,000-meter steeplechase. Amos Biwott won the gold, while the silver medal went to Benjamin Kogo.

In Mexico City, Kenyan runners took the experts by surprise. Never before had athletes from that country challenged in the Olympics. Many experts claimed that the Kenyans did so well in 1968 only because they were accustomed to running in high altitudes.

The 1972 Olympics were held in the low altitudes of Munich, Germany. Again the Kenyans dominated the distance races. The great Kipchoge Keino initiated the heroics by placing second in the 1,500 meters. Then Keino thrilled Olympic fans with a record-breaking performance in the 3,000-meter steeplechase. His teammate Ben Jipcho finished second in that race. For the second straight Olympic games, Kenyan runners had finished first and second in the punishing steeplechase event. The team from Kenya also won the 1,600-meter relay race that year.

Many people feel that sports and politics do not mix. However, it has not always been easy to keep politics out of the sporting arena. Kenya and several other African governments refused to permit their athletes to compete in the 1976 Olympics in protest against South Africa's racial policies. The nation also boycotted the 1980 Olympics in Moscow to protest Russia's invasion of Afghanistan. President Jimmy Carter kept the United States out of that Olympiad for the same reason. So for two Olympiads, the fans of distance running were unable to see Kenya's latest group of fleet-footed athletes.

Mr. Soi's Olympics poster honors Kenya's remarkable distance runners.

One of the country's newest distance runners is Henry Rono, a Nandi who comes from the Great Rift Valley. In 1978, Rono smashed three world track records. Running in Oslo, Vienna, and Seattle, Rono set new marks in the 3,000-meter race, the 10,000-meter race, and the 3,000-meter steeplechase. No distance runner has ever scored so many records in one year. Had he been allowed to compete, the 1980 Olympics would certainly have been Rono's showcase.

Boycotts plagued the 1984 Olympics, as the Soviet Union and other Communist-bloc nations refused to participate. This time, however, the Kenyan team journeyed to Los Angeles to compete in Kenya's first Olympics in twelve years. Its performance was an enormous disappointment. Kenyan runners failed to win a single major track event. In Kenya, where track is followed passionately by sports lovers, a feeling of gloom hung over the land for months afterward.

In Tsavo National Park,
tourists can get a
close-up view of some
of the park's thousands
of elephants (above),
or join a safari tour,
which may include fording
one of the park's
many streams (right).

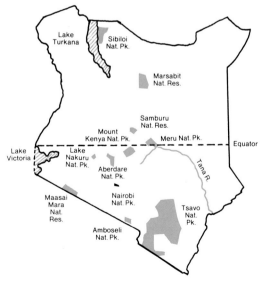

Chapter 7
THE NATIONAL
PARK SYSTEM

When world travelers think of Kenya, they automatically picture herds of wild animals roaming over endless flowing grasslands. The image is correct. Kenya is a treasure chest of African wildlife. But if that wealth of wildlife is not protected from the abuses of man, it will vanish forever. In order to preserve its wildlife, Kenya has developed a magnificent system of national parks.

More than 10 percent of Kenya's total land area is devoted to national parks and wildlife reserves. There are some forty parks and game reserves in the country. Five of the most important are Nairobi, Tsavo, Mount Kenya, Lake Nakuru, and Aberdare national parks.

NAIROBI NATIONAL PARK

Nairobi, the capital of Kenya, is a modern, bustling city of almost one million people. Yet only ten minutes away, uncaged lions lounge in the sun after feasting on a meal of wild zebra. No

Only ten minutes away from the capital city (background), wild animals are free to roam in Nairobi National Park.

other city in Africa, or for that matter in the rest of the world, can boast a wildlife sanctuary almost in the shadow of its high-rise buildings.

Nairobi National Park, covering 44 square miles (114 square kilometers), is small by Kenyan standards. The tall cyclone fence enclosing it keeps the animals inside and the illegal hunters outside. Tourists visit the park in buses. The one rule: Stay inside the buses. Although the lions often look lazy, they can be dangerous. In addition to lions, the park has rhinoceros, giraffes, zebras, antelope, and a variety of monkeys. Large baboons sometimes leap from the tree branches onto the rooftops of tourist buses. They cling to the luggage carriers and have to be chased away.

TSAVO NATIONAL PARK

The greatest stock of wild animals in all of Kenya is found in Tsavo National Park. Spreading over more than 8,000 square miles (20,720 square kilometers), Tsavo is one of the largest wild

The termite hills in Tsavo National Park are homes for huge insect populations.

animal reserves in the world. Established in 1948, the park is divided into two distinct areas. Tsavo East is relatively flat and covered by grasses and thorn trees. Though the grasslands there can appear drab and parched after a long period of drought, the fields burst into flower after the slightest rain. Tsavo West, largely made up of volcanic rock, is dotted with springs and water holes.

When journalist Allan Fisher camped out at Tsavo, he recorded this impression: "First dawn at Tsavo National Park. Something soundless but compelling awakens me. I do not understand, but I know I must go to the door of my tent. Not forty yards away, his bulk a gray cliff against the light, a huge bull elephant grazes. . . .He sees me, takes a step in my direction. Then perhaps he senses my admiration and good will, stronger even than my fear. The grazing continues; we feel comfortable with one another. Finally, he ambles off."

Water holes in Tsavo National Park attract an amazing variety of wildlife.

Estimates place Tsavo's wild elephants at twenty thousand. Most of the country's black rhinoceros live there, too, as do buffalo, zebras, giraffes, lions, leopards, cheetahs, and many species of antelope.

Though the government provides tours of this huge park, it would be impossible to see more than a fraction of its marvels on a tour. So park officials have arranged for the animals to visit the tourists. Lodges with water holes and salt licks nearby have been built in the bush. Tourists can sit in the lodges and watch the wild animals roaming free. Some of the lodges are enclosed by bars and have the effect of a zoo in reverse—the people are kept in cages so they cannot disturb the animals.

This mountain-climbing party is making camp on the slopes of Mount Kenya.

MOUNT KENYA NATIONAL PARK

Kenya's highest national park encompasses the soaring peaks of Mount Kenya. The park begins at the height of 11,000 feet (3,353 meters) above sea level and then sweeps still higher. Bamboo trees stand on some slopes, but most of the park is too high to support anything but cactus and shrubs. Partly because of the startlingly clear air at these dizzying, windswept altitudes, the views are spectacular. Tourists need not fear encountering dangerous animals at these heights; wild animals simply refuse to climb so high.

Truly determined hikers join mountain-climbing parties and struggle up the highest peaks of Mount Kenya. Park animals called zebroids often accompany the parties as far as the snow line. A zebroid is a cross between a horse or donkey and a zebra. At the higher altitudes, climbers have snowball fights so they can later boast that they have thrown snowballs while standing very near the equator.

LAKE NAKURU NATIONAL PARK

Situated in the Great Rift Valley about a hundred miles (161 kilometers) northwest of Nairobi is heart-shaped Lake Nakuru. Many ornithologists (bird experts) consider it to be the site of the finest bird spectacle on earth. The 18-square-mile (47-square-kilometer) lake attracts more migrating flamingos than any other body of water on the planet. The long-legged birds feed on the algae that grow in the lake waters. At peak season, more than a million flamingos gather in this lake alone.

Flamingos are not the only spectacle in the park. Some three hundred species of birds also live along the shores of the lake. The park is a bird-lover's paradise.

ABERDARE NATIONAL PARK

In Kenya's highlands, about a two-hour drive from Nairobi, lies Aberdare National Park. Spreading to the southwest of Mount Kenya, this mountain park displays the surprising variety of Kenya's highland landscapes. The park boasts mountain rain forests, bamboo thickets, and extensive marshland. Nearly every species of Kenya's wild-animal population can be found in Aberdare, including thousands of chattering monkeys.

A unique tourist attraction found in the park is a hotel called Treetops. Built in the branches of an enormous Cape Chestnut tree, the hotel offers its guests a rare view of wildlife. The front veranda of Treetops overlooks a small lake and a salt lick that serve as a magnet for animals. Floodlights illuminate the lake shores at night and tourists can enjoy dinner while watching wild animals calmly feeding below. The hotel invites its guests to note

One view of the Treetops hotel in Aberdare National Park, where visitors can watch animals at the lake below as they eat their dinner on the veranda

the number of animals seen during the course of a dinner. Said author Robert S. Kane, "Yes, you *are* indeed given a score card, and I kept one from my last visit: One elephant, two rhinoceros, ninety-five buffalo, seventeen warthogs, four hyenas, thirty-five waterbucks, fourteen bush bucks. And in between one enjoys a six-course dinner with wine."

The Treetops hotel was once the site of a curious twist of history. In 1952, a very special tourist, Princess Elizabeth of England, climbed to a top room to spend an evening. That same night, thousands of miles away in Great Britain, her father, King George VI, died in his sleep. The next morning when she climbed down to earth again, the very special tourist had become England's Queen Elizabeth II.

Though it is illegal to kill a wild animal anywhere in Kenya, poachers find ways to hunt crocodiles for their hides, leopards for their skins, and elephants for their valuable ivory tusks.

POLICING THE NATIONAL PARKS

The wild animals of Kenya are tempting targets for the country's throngs of poor people. It is illegal to kill a wild animal anywhere in Kenya. Still, illegal hunting, or poaching, remains a serious problem. Poor Africans living in the rural areas look upon a wild zebra as meat, not as the national asset the government insists it is. In addition to meat, animals provide other riches for poachers. Leopard skins can be sold to dealers, who in turn make them into fashionable coats. Ivory from elephant tusks is extremely valuable. The tough hide of crocodiles is sold to shoemakers, who work it into expensive boots. Selling these wild animal products is illegal, but an underground trade flourishes nevertheless. Most of these illegal goods are sold abroad.
To conduct their secret hunts, poachers sneak into areas with the greatest concentrations of wild animals—usually national parks.

Poachers sell rhinoceros horn to customers in China and India.

These huge parks have many remote areas in which poachers can go about their illegal business undetected.

Game wardens employed by the national park system are heroic in their efforts to track down poachers. But the parks are enormous, the game wardens are few, and the poachers are crafty. Poachers seeking skins have reduced the leopard nearly to extinction in Kenya. Rhinoceros are also on the endangered list. In China and India, an ancient belief holds that ground rhinoceros horn can rejuvenate the powers of the elderly. To meet the demand for this powder, poachers shoot rhinoceros, remove their horns, and leave the animals to rot in the grasses.

Kenya's national park system has accomplished miracles in its goal to preserve the nation's wildlife. But government officials agree that an even greater effort is needed as poverty drives more and more Kenyans into a life of preying on the wild animals in order to earn a living.

Those who travel widely in Africa have learned to appreciate the efficiency of the modern nation of Kenya, where the airlines, banks, and mails work and where new movies, books, and an abundance of fresh produce are available.

Chapter 8

THE CHALLENGE OF
MODERN KENYA

As Kenya entered the 1980s, diplomats around the world hailed it as black Africa's model state. True, ethnic rivalries still existed, but since independence the fabric of the nation had held firm. Kenya functioned the way a modern state should. Writing in 1981, veteran photojournalist Marion Kaplan said, "Those of us who traveled widely in other African countries, and became fraught and frazzled [with] the bureaucratic frustrations and daily challenges of trying to get a story or take a picture, would return to Kenya with relief. There things worked: the airways, the mails, the banks, the service stations, the grocery stores. There were new movies, good books, green vegetables, fresh cream."

Kenya of the early 1980s was also a marvelous example of racial harmony in a continent where racism often reigned. As Marion Kaplan reported: "[In Kenya] I photographed blacks, whites, and browns on golf courses. . .in the streets and hotel terraces, in friends' houses. An African dentist agreed to my doing a picture with his white nurse. By chance, when I went to do the picture, the patient in the chair was Asian."

In the early 1980s, Kenya was the only African nation that had a flying doctor service.

World leaders pointed out that the government of Kenya was genuinely concerned with the problems and sufferings of people. The government's commitment to education and national health was praised. Of all African nations, only Kenya had a flying doctor service that flew teams of medics in light planes into remote areas. Previously, these regions had had to rely on traditional diviners for health care.

But this image of stability and harmony was shattered during a seventy-two-hour outburst of violence that began on August 1, 1982.

THE ATTEMPTED MILITARY TAKEOVER

"The magic that was Kenya disappeared on a Sunday morning," said Peter Frank, manager of the Hilton Hotel in downtown Nairobi. On that morning, bursts of gunfire announced a military coup. Amid confusion and bloodshed, a group of discontented members of the nation's air force declared that they had deposed the government of President Daniel arap Moi and had taken over Kenya. The airmen circulated handbills claiming that their actions were justified because "rampant corruption and nepotism have made life almost impossible in our society. The economy is in shambles and the people can't afford food, housing, and transport."

Almost immediately after the announced takeover, hundreds of students at the University of Nairobi joined the rebel airmen. Next, hordes of ragged shantytown dwellers rampaged through the downtown streets smashing shop windows, looting goods, and rifling cash registers. One eyewitness told a *Time* magazine reporter, "Guys were running around stuffing money into their pants, and when their pockets were full, they stuffed the money in their underpants."

From the start, the attempted power grab was a clumsy operation. Within six hours, loyal soldiers of the nation's army captured most of the airmen who had revolted. The others fled to Tanzania. President Moi ordered the arrest of almost every man in his 2,200-member air force.

Even after the leaders of the coup had been arrested, street rioting continued. For the next three days, the desperately poor shantytown dwellers battled with police. Many university students joined the melee. Before order was restored, 129 Kenyans were dead and another 100 were missing.

Time magazine gave this grim account of the aftermath of the rioting: "The sense of strain and anxiety lingered ominously. Banks and government offices were open, but workers and shoppers who normally thronged the downtown streets of Nairobi were rushing for home by mid-afternoon to observe a dusk-to-dawn curfew, leaving the city center a ghost town. Blocks of shops in the downtown area were boarded up, concealing the shattered windows and vacant shelves left by an orgy of looting. Occasionally, corpses could be seen on the city streets, evidence that a tough government crackdown was still in progress in one of Africa's most pro-Western and pro-capitalistic countries."

KENYA'S DESPERATE POVERTY

The attempted military takeover and the rioting that followed illustrated to the world that frightening problems tear at the heart of what is often called black Africa's most successful society. Crushing poverty is the most overwhelming problem the country faces. In the shantytowns that ring Nairobi, people live in huts and lean-tos built of cardboard and scrap wood. Whole families search through garbage heaps looking for something to sell for food money. The countryside also has been stricken by poverty. Kenyans are a largely rural people. Only 15 percent of the population lives in the cities. In the rural areas, a slight lack of rainfall can mean widespread famine. Many rural people refuse even to consider uprooting themselves and going to the cities in search of jobs. They know that in the cities their plight would be even worse.

Poverty without the hope of a better life can crack even the proudest people. Writer Allan Fisher, touring Maasailand, said: "Out in the bush I have seen Maasai beg money from tourists with harsh cries of *'Shillingi! Shillingi!'* (Shilling! Shilling!). I once watched a tourist with a movie camera pay villagers to form a circle, join hands, and jump up and down with wild yells—the tourist's idea of a Maasai dance. The Maasai laughed, but I couldn't."

Though Kenya is often called black Africa's most successful society, crushing poverty remains an overwhelming problem and shantytowns such as this one surround the city of Nairobi.

Kenya's ranks of poor are steadily growing. The country has become impoverished mainly because there are too many people and not enough farmland. The birthrate of a country is determined by the number of births per one hundred people in a year. Kenya's birthrate is 3.9 percent, which many experts believe is the world's highest. By contrast, the birthrate in the United States is .7 percent. Kenyans believe it is important to have large families. In the past the nation's farmland, though limited, managed to feed all of the people. But the population has doubled since independence. The farms cannot begin to grow enough crops to feed the present population of twenty million.

Kenya's highly productive farms flourish only in the highlands and the Great Rift Valley. In the rest of the nation, rainfall is too scant to grow bountiful crops. Poor soil and lack of rainfall render about 80 percent of Kenya's total land area useless for farming. Because of the increasing population and limited farm production, Kenya must import grain and corn from foreign countries. These

109

items are a costly expenditure for a nation that exports few products. During the 1980s, Kenya's national debt rose at the rate of almost one billion dollars a year. In turn, the average Kenyan earns only about four hundred dollars a year. And even that meager figure is dropping.

KENYA'S FUTURE

Despite the country's economic problems, Kenya continues to make progress in other areas. The government's commitment to education is paying dividends. More and more technicians, farm managers, doctors, and engineers are Kenya born and educated. In the past, such highly trained men and women either came from foreign lands or were Kenyans educated in Europe or America.

In modern Kenya, the rivalries among ethnic groups have been kept under control. Ever since independence, so-called experts have predicted that internal warfare would tear the country apart. But the only large-scale conflicts occurred in 1982, and they were caused by the frustrations of poverty and were unrelated to ethnic rivalry. If anything, ethnic tensions have lessened in recent years. Democratic education, which brings children of various culture groups together in classrooms, has contributed to the easing of such tensions.

Tourism is a bright note in Kenya's economic picture. Every year, hordes of foreign tourists flock to this marvelous land. The tourists enjoy meeting with the genuinely friendly people, viewing the spectacular scenery, and observing the fascinating wildlife. Because it creates jobs and goodwill, the national government promotes tourism. The *Kenya Safari Guide,* an official government pamphlet, urges visitors to come to the country

Tanzania's Mount Kilimanjaro (above), the highest mountain in Africa, is one of the spectacular scenic views that can be seen from Kenya.

because "there are shimmering plains, dotted with thorn trees and teeming with game; there are mountain forests with green glades and cool brooks; there are rich and verdant highlands. There is something for everyone: photographers, writers, sportsmen, painters, fishermen, climbers, divers, and, of course, those who like to laze around in the sun midst exotic surroundings." Kenya is one of the few countries whose government tourist promotions are not mere propaganda. The land is as exciting as the government claims it to be.

What does the future hold for Kenya? A gloomy economic picture shrouds most of black Africa. In recent years, Africa has suffered from the effects of the worldwide economic slowdown. A persistent, devastating drought has ravaged the crops of Kenya and her neighbors.

Still, the spirits of the people remain high. Kenyans admit their society has faults. Yet they join hands and proudly sing out their word for unity, strength, and peace—*Harambee! Harambee! Harambee!*

MAP KEY

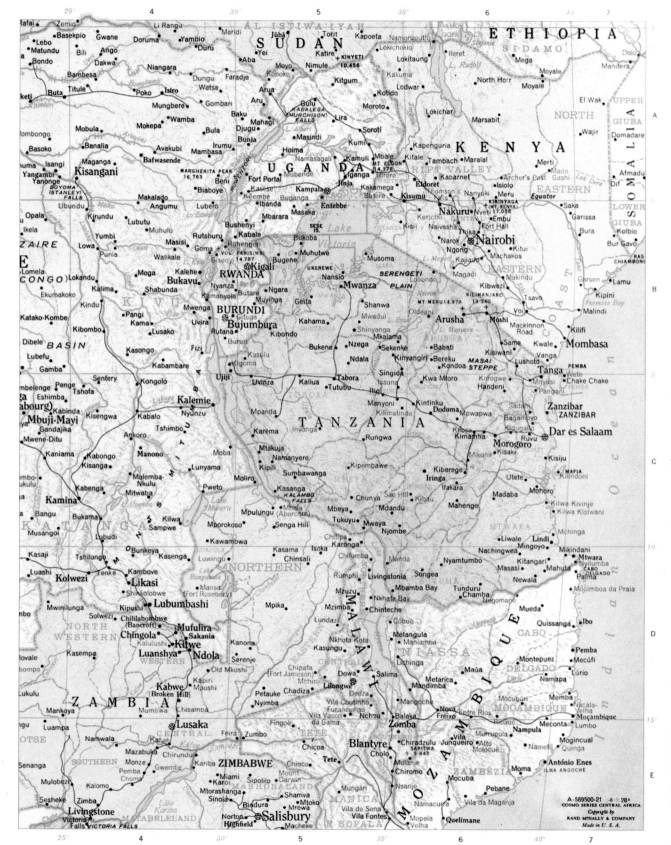

MINI-FACTS AT A GLANCE

GENERAL INFORMATION

Official Name: *Jamhuri ya Kenya* (Republic of Kenya)

Capital: Nairobi

Official Language: Swahili

Other Languages: English; local languages or dialects spoken by various ethnic groups

Government: Kenya is a republic. Its president is elected by the people to a five-year term. The legislature, called the National Assembly, is made up of 170 members, 158 of whom are elected to five-year terms and 12 of whom are appointed by the president. The president selects the vice-president and about 20 cabinet ministers from among members of the assembly. Each cabinet minister heads a department of government.
Kenya is divided into seven provinces. These provinces are further divided into forty rural districts. Each district is headed by a presidentially appointed commissioner. Nairobi is a separate district.

Flag: The national flag of Kenya has three wide horizontal stripes of black, red, and green that are separated by two narrow white stripes. The black stripe symbolizes the Kenyan people, the red stripe their struggle for independence, and the green stripe agriculture. In the center of the flag, a red shield with black and white markings lies upon a pair of crossed white spears, signifying the defense of freedom.

Coat of Arms: The coat of arms bears two lions and the Swahili word *harambee*, which means "pulling together."

National Song: *"Wimbo wa Taifa"* ("Anthem of the Nation")

Religion: More than half of Kenya's people are Christians. Two thirds of those Christians are Protestant, the rest Roman Catholic. About 40 percent of the people practice traditional African religions, and about 5 percent are Islamic.

Money: The basic unit of money is the Kenya shilling. It is divided into one hundred cents. Twenty Kenya shillings make up a Kenyan pound. In 1985, one U.S. dollar was worth fifteen Kenya shillings.

Weights and Measures: Kenya uses the metric system.

Population: 23,338,000 (1988 estimate). Distribution is 81 percent rural, 19 percent urban. The density is 104 persons per sq. mi. (40 persons per km²).

Cities:

Nairobi 827,775
Mombasa 341,148
Kisumu 152,643
Nakuru 92,851
Thika 41,324

(Population figures according to the 1988 estimate)

GEOGRAPHY

Borders: Countries that border Kenya are Ethiopia on the north, Somalia on the east, Tanzania on the southwest, Uganda on the west, and Sudan on the northwest.

Highest Point: Mount Kenya, 17,058 ft. (5,199 m)

Lowest Point: Sea level

Coastline: 300 mi. (483 km)

Rivers: Kenya's chief rivers are the Tana, 500 mi. (805 km) long, and the Athi, 200 mi. (322 km) long. Both rivers flow from the highlands to the Indian Ocean. The eastern part of the Athi is called the Galana.

Lakes: The largest lake lying within Kenya's borders is Lake Turkana, called Lake Rudolf in Ethiopia. Kenya shares Lake Victoria, Africa's largest lake, with Uganda and Tanzania.

Climate: Although the equator runs through Kenya, not all of the country is hot. Altitude, not proximity to the equator, determines temperatures in Kenya. The country has two rainy seasons, the "long rains" from April to June, and the "short rains" from October to December.
    There are three climatic regions in Kenya—the tropical coast, the dry plains, and the fertile highlands. The coastal region is hot and humid all year long. Average rainfall is about 40 in. (102 cm) per year. Average temperatures are about 80°F. (27°C). The plains, or savannas, cover about three fourths of the country. This is the driest and most thinly populated area of Kenya. Some sections receive only 10 to 30 in. (25 to 76 cm) of rain per year. The altitude determines temperatures in this area. At higher elevations, the average temperature is about 60°F. (16°C). At low elevations, it is 80°F. (27°C). The highlands, which lie in southwestern Kenya, cover about one fourth of the country. This is a fertile region of mountains, valleys, and plateaus. Rainfall is abundant, ranging from 40 to 50 in. (102 to 127 cm) per year. Temperatures average about 67°F. (19°C). Because the highlands provide a good climate for agriculture, it is Kenya's chief farming region.

The natural hot springs near Lake Bagoria spout fountains of boiling water.

Greatest Distances: North to south—640 mi. (1,030 km)
East to west—560 mi. (901 km)

Area: 224,961 sq. mi. (582, 647 km²)

NATURE

Vegetation: There is a large variety of plant life in Kenya. Along the coast are groves of coconut palms, cashew trees, mangrove trees, and other tropical plant life. There are also a few small rain forests in this area. Short grasses, bushes, and thorn trees (acacias) grow on the plains, as well as candelabra and baobab trees. The highlands have grasslands, alpine meadows, and rich forests. The most common trees there are African camphor, African olive, and pencil cedar. Bamboo trees grow on the mountains.

Animals: Elephants, monkeys, lions, leopards, zebras, antelopes, giraffes, and cheetahs, as well as many other exotic animals, are found on the savannas and in the highlands. Hippopotamuses, crocodiles, and rhinoceros can be found near the lagoons and swamps. Many varieties of snakes live on the ground and in trees.

Birds: Crowned cranes, ostriches, flamingos, Egyptian geese, herons, starlings, and spoonbills

Fish: Starfish, stonefish, jellyfish, zebra fish, parrot fish, sea urchins, and the red fire fish are found off the coast of Kenya.

National Parks: To protect its wildlife, Kenya has established some forty national parks and reserves. About two dozen of these are equipped to handle tourists. The parks cover 13,514 sq. mi. (35,000 km²), or 10 percent of Kenya's total landmass.

Tsavo National Park, spreading over more than 8,000 sq. mi. (20,720 km²), has the greatest stock of wild animals in all of Kenya, and is one of the largest wild animal reserves in the world. *Nairobi National Park* is unusual because although it is small by Kenyan standards, covering only 44 sq. mi. (114 km²), it is practically in the backyard of the bustling capital city of Nairobi. *Mount Kenya National Park,* which begins at a height of 11,000 ft. (3,353 m) and encompasses the soaring peaks of Mount Kenya, offers spectacular views. Situated in the highlands is *Aberdare National Park,* where nearly every species of Kenya's wild-animal population can be found. Aberdare is also the site of Kenya's famous Treetops hotel. Other important national parks are *Amboseli National Park, Lake Nakuru National Park, Maasai Mara Game Reserve, Marsabit National Park, Meru National Park, Samburu National Reserve,* and *Sibiloi National Park.*

In order to preserve the magnificent marine life off the coast of Kenya, four areas of coastline have been designated marine national parks or reserves. They are *Malindi Marine Park, Watamu Marine Park, Kisite-Mpunguti Marine Park,* and *Kiunga National Marine Reserve.* Snorkeling is permitted at the marine parks and reserves, but no one is allowed to fish or remove coral or shells.

EVERYDAY LIFE

Food: The staple food of Kenyans is maize (corn), which is milled into flour and made into a porridge called *posho.* It is sometimes served with a beef stew called *ngali. Irio* is *posho* mixed with mashed beans, potatoes, and other vegetables. Also popular in Kenya is a steamed banana porridge called *matoke.*

Housing: In rural areas, most Kenyans live in small, thatched-roof houses with dirt floors and walls made of mud or bundles of branches. Most urban Kenyans live in houses or apartment buildings made of stone or cement.

Holidays:
> January 1 (New Year's Day)
> Easter
> May 1 (Labour Day)
> June 1 (Madaraka Day, anniversary of self-government)
> June 30 (*Id ul Fitr,* end of Ramadan)
> September 6 (*Id ul Adha,* Feast of the Sacrifice)
> October 20 (Kenyatta Day)
> December 12 (Independence Day)
> December 25-26 (Christmas)

Culture: Much of Kenya's art is inspired by religion. Through sculpture, music, dance, and literature, the Kenyan seeks to appeal to the spirit world. Sculpture is the most highly developed of all African art forms. To ward off evil spirits and attract good ones, diviners sometimes give clients intricately carved amulets or charms. Kenyans also sculpt larger figures in ivory or gold. Wood carving is a widely respected art form in Kenya. Wood figures of ancestors have religious significance and are favorite subjects for carvers.

Traditional literature in Kenya is mainly oral and consists of folktales. The folktales may involve man's encounters with spirits, or they may be war stories praising ancient heroes.

In recent years, Kenyans have become interested in Western music, classical as well as modern. Yet they still revere their own traditional music, which is characterized by strong and intricate rhythms. Singing and dancing are very much a part of their music. Kenyan music utilizes drums, lutes, woodwinds, and other instruments. The complex music is polyrhythmic, which means that different instruments and singers play different rhythms at the same time.

The dance is a highly respected art form in Kenya. Traditionally, dances have had a religious function. While performing these dances, Kenyans wear highly stylized headdresses and masks that are decorated with feathers and painted with brilliant colors.

Sports and Recreation: Soccer, a British import, is the most popular team sport in Kenya. The country also has produced some exceptional tennis players. But Kenya is best known in the sports world for its distance runners. Kenyan runners first became internationally prominent in the 1968 Olympic games in Mexico City. They also dominated the distance races at the 1972 Olympic games in Munich.

Schools: Although school is not compulsory in Kenya, education is highly valued by Kenyan parents, and about 80 percent of Kenyan children receive at least an elementary education. Primary school in Kenya is a seven-year course. Only the first four years are free of charge. Beyond that, parents must pay a modest tuition fee. The country suffers from a severe shortage of secondary schools. Children in remote areas of the country are at a disadvantage because the schools are concentrated mostly in urban and highly populated areas. To help alleviate this problem, groups of private citizens have set up self-help *(harambee)* schools in some places where no government schools exist.

The University of Nairobi, with about nine thousand students, is Kenya's largest school of higher education. There are also about ten other colleges in the country, including some that offer training in specialized subjects such as agriculture or education.

Health: Kenya has a partially socialized health care system. This means that the government runs the hospitals and other medical services. Medical attention is available for anyone who needs it. A flying doctor service takes care of those in rural areas, and private organizations such as missions and private charities also provide medical care.

Lentils and beans are among the staple foods in Kenya.

ECONOMY AND INDUSTRY

Principal Products:
Agriculture: Coffee, corn, sisal, wheat, meat, sugarcane, tea
Manufacturing: Cement, chemicals, light machinery, textiles, processed foods, petroleum products

Communication: Five major daily newspapers, three in English and two in Swahili, are published in Nairobi. Kenya also has approximately fifty periodicals. A government-owned network, The Voice of Kenya, broadcasts radio programs for 285 hours per week in nineteen different languages, including Swahili, English, Arabic, and many local languages. About thirty-eight hours per week of television programming are provided to the Nairobi and Kisumu areas. Kenyans own about 1.5 million radios and 100,000 television sets.

Transportation: There are about 29,400 mi. (47,315 km) of roads in Kenya, although only 2,400 mi. (3,862 km) are paved. About 1,200 mi. (1,930 km) of railways connect the major cities and towns. A country-wide bus service connects rural and urban areas.

There are international airports at Nairobi and Mombasa, and smaller airports in Kisumu and Malindi. Kenya also has about 166 airstrips.

Mombasa is a fully equipped international port that is served by the regular shipping lines, and there is steamship service on Lake Victoria.

IMPORTANT DATES

A.D. 500 — Bantu speakers occupy the Congo River Valley

A.D. 900s — Arab merchants establish outposts along the African coast

1498 — Vasco Da Gama, the first European to round the Cape of Good Hope, arrives at Mombasa

1590s — The Portuguese build Fort Jesus on Mombasa Island

1849 — Johann Ludwig Krapf becomes the first European to discover Mount Kenya

1856 — Richard Francis Burton and John Hanning Speke begin search for source of the Nile River

1858 — John Speke discovers Lake Victoria

1884-85 — Conference of Berlin held to establish the way in which European countries will divide Africa

1895 — The British begin building a railroad connecting Mombasa and Lake Victoria; they establish the East African Protectorate

1905 — War between the British and the Nandi

1920 — Kenya becomes a British colony

1921 — Harry Thuku, a Kikuyu, establishes a protest group called the East Africa Association

1944 — The Kenya African Union, a nationalist political party, founded

1946 — Jomo Kenyatta returns to Kenya after sixteen years in England

1947 — Kenyatta elected president of the Kenya African Union

1952 — King George VI of England dies while his daughter is visiting Kenya; she becomes Queen Elizabeth II

1952-56 — Mau Mau uprisings

1953 — Kenyatta convicted of leading the Mau Mau movement and sent to prison for nine years

1957 — Black Africans elect eight representatives to the colonial legislature

1961—Blacks win the majority of seats in the legislature; Kenyatta released from prison and assumes control of the Kenya African National Union, the Dominant political party

1963—Kenya gains independence

1964—Kenyatta becomes president of the new republic

1966—Oginga Odinga tries to form his own political party; he is arrested and all political parties except the Kenya African National Union are banned

1968—Kenyan runners take top honors at the Olympics in Mexico City

1969—Political leader Tom Mboya assassinated

1972—Kenyan runners dominate the distance races at the Olympics in Munich

1978—Jomo Kenyatta dies; Vice-President Daniel arap Moi becomes acting president; Moi elected president

1982—Unsuccessful military coup

1983—Moi reelected president

1985—A 2½-million-year-old skull, challenging widely held beliefs about human ancestors, is discovered near Lake Turkana

IMPORTANT PEOPLE

Joy Adamson (1910-1980), British naturalist and author who lived in Kenya for many years and wrote several books, including *Born Free*, about her experiences there

Amos Biwott, Kenyan runner and 1968 Olympic gold medalist in the 3,000-meter steeplechase

Karen Blixen (pen name Isak Dinesen) (1885-1962), Danish author and Kenya pioneer who wrote *Out of Africa*, a memoir of her experiences as owner of a coffee plantation in Kenya's highlands

Sir Richard Francis Burton (1821-1890), British explorer who joined John Hanning Speke on a search for the source of the Nile River

Vasco Da Gama (1469?-1524), Portuguese sea captain and explorer who was the first European to round the Cape of Good Hope at the southern tip of Africa

Sir Charles Norton Edgcumbe Eliot (1862-1931), early British governor of Kenya

Ben Jipcho, Kenyan runner and 1972 Olympic silver medalist in the 3,000-meter steeplechase

Kipchoge Keino, Kenyan runner and Olympic champion; won gold medals in the 1,500-meter race in 1968 and the 3,000-meter steeplechase in 1972; won silver medals in the 5,000-meter race in 1968 and the 1,500-meter race in 1972

Jomo Kenyatta (1890?-1978), leader of Kenyan nationalist movement during Kenya's colonial period and first president of independent Kenya

Benjamin Kogo, Kenyan runner and 1968 Olympic silver medalist in the 3,000-meter steeplechase

Johann Ludwig Krapf (1810-1881), German explorer who was the first European to discover Mount Kenya

Louis S.B. Leakey (1903-1972), British anthropologist who made important discoveries in Kenya concerning the origins of mankind; proved that human evolution was centered in Africa, not in Asia

Mary Nicol Leakey (1913-   ), British anthropologist and wife of Louis Leakey; assisted her husband in important fossil discoveries in Kenya's Great Rift Valley

Richard Leakey (1944-   ), British anthropologist and son of Louis and Mary Leakey; his discoveries in Kenya pushed back many anthropologists' estimates of the beginning date of human evolution; administrative director of the National Museum of Kenya

David Livingstone (1813-1873), British missionary and explorer of Africa

Lord Frederick John Dealtry Lugard, first Baron Lugard (1858-1945), British soldier and colonial administrator who visited Kenya at the end of the nineteeth century

Tom Mboya (1930-1969), Kenyan labor leader, politician, and spokesman for Kenyan independence; cabinet minister under President Jomo Kenyatta

Daniel T. arap Moi (1924-   ), current president of Kenya

Oginga Odinga (1911-   ), political opposition leader in early days of Kenyan independence; first vice-president of Kenya

Pablo Picasso (1881-1973), Spanish artist who was influenced by African wood carvings

Ptolemy (Claudius Ptolemaeus) (second century A.D.), Greek geographer who correctly believed that the Nile had two sources

Johannes Rebmann (1820-1876), German missionary and explorer of East Africa, discovered Mount Kilimanjaro with Ludwig Krapf

Henry Rono, Kenyan runner who smashed three world records in 1978

Tepilit Ole Saitoti, Kenyan author of *Maasai*, a book about the history and culture of the Maasai people

John Hanning Speke (1827-1864), British explorer who in his search for the source of the Nile River became the first European to discover Lake Victoria

Sir Henry Morton Stanley (1841-1904), British journalist and explorer of Africa

Naftali Temu, Kenyan runner, 1968 Olympic gold medalist in the 10,000-meter race and bronze medalist in the 5,000-meter race

Harry Thuku (1895-1970), early spokesman for Kenyan independence; in 1921 established a protest group called the East Africa Association

A group of zebras, a greater kudu, and an elephant share a water hole.

INDEX

Page numbers that appear in boldface type indicate illustrations

About the Author

R. Conrad Stein was born and grew up in Chicago. He enlisted in the Marine Corps at the age of eighteen and served for three years. He then attended the University of Illinois where he received a Bachelor's degree in history. He later studied in Mexico, earning an advanced degree from the University of Guanajuato. Mr. Stein is the author of many other books, articles, and short stories written for young people.

Mr. Stein is married to Deborah Kent, who is also a writer of books for young readers. They have a daughter, Janna.